Reader Testimonies

Since publishing Waking Up, Terry Wise has become perhaps the most prominent voice of suicide attempt survivors in mental health and suicide prevention in the United States...Anyone who has read her engrossing book or heard her speak can testify that Terry's inspiring story is not one that can easily be forgotten, and her messages for finding help and hope are words to live by.

John Draper, Ph.D., Executive Director, National Suicide Prevention
Lifeline, 800-273-TALK (8255)

As a member of the faculty of Harvard Medical School I have recommended Waking Up for the reading list and also as a selection for the faculty at the Massachusetts General Hospital.

Lyn M. Duncan, M.D., Harvard Medical School, Professor

In her book, in her talks, in the example of her own life, I am convinced that Terry saves lives and pulls people out of the darkness that envelopes them.

Rabbi Harold Kushner, Author,
When Bad Things Happen to Good People

Rarely has [the therapeutic process] been so vividly depicted by a client...Anyone seeking to understand what an effective therapy is really about would do well to read this beautifully written memoir.

Rutgers University, Nancy McWilliams, Ph.D.,
Professor and Author of *Psychoanalytic Psychotherapy:*
A Practitioner's Guide

A public speaker, teacher, and model for recovery... [Terry] is an extraordinary and compelling presenter.

American Association of Suicidology, Lanny Berman, Ph.D., Executive Director and Author of *Comprehensive Textbook of Suicidology*; Professor, American University

Waking Up is required reading in two of my courses... It is the best written account of long-term psychotherapy.

Columbia University, Barry Farber, Ph.D., Director, Counseling and Clinical Psychology

[Terry is] one of the rare speakers who combines her personal experience with an understanding of the literature...Articulate and compelling [Wise] is a gift to all of us coping with death and grief...Despite my having been a practicing therapist for many years now, Waking Up stimulated new thinking and ways of understanding the therapeutic process for me. Terry's story is captivating as well as educational.

Carol Wogrin, Psy.D., R.N., Director, National Center for Death Education

For those in the helping professions, this book is a must read... For those struggling with depression and suicidal thoughts, [Waking Up] is a reminder that even when you think it impossible, you can find a reason for living.

M. David Rudd, Ph.D., Past President, American Association of Suicidology and Author of *Treating Suicidal Behavior*

A breathtakingly honest account...a true testament that child abuse does not end when the touching stops.

Prevent Child Abuse America, A. Sidney Johnson III, President

I just completed Waking Up and I just want you to know you saved my life...I decided to stay alive one more day so I could re-read it, and today the urge is not present. Thank you.

Anonymous

I am an incest survivor...[Waking Up] has encouraged me to reach out once again and try to find the help I need to deal with these feelings...Thank you for having the courage to write.

Anonymous

Wise doesn't just captivate you from the first page... she holds you by the gut and pulls you into her life (and death) experience...she [opened up her soul] with the hopes that it would make a difference for others. Well, in this reader's case, she succeeded.

Anonymous

About the Author

Widowed at 35 following her husband's death from Lou Gehrig's Disease (ALS), and after surviving a near-fatal suicide attempt, Terry Wise spent the next several years in treatment. A former Boston trial attorney, Wise has since devoted her life to international public speaking and full-time writing (www. TerryWise.com). She has traveled to hundreds of cities to appear as a keynote speaker, continuing education instructor and workshop presenter, speaking to both the general public and professionals on topics related to depression, grief, long-term caregiving, suicide prevention, and the process of recovery.

Wise is the recipient of a *National Mental Health Award* for "distinguished work that has had a major impact on the depression community." She makes frequent media appearances and is a featured speaker on a National Award-Winning educational video sponsored by the U.S. Department of Health and Human Services, Substance Abuse & Mental Health Services Administration (SAMHSA). She is also the featured interview on WebMD's *"Depression Insights"* Video Series. Wise serves on the boards of numerous organizations, including the American Association of Suicidology, Families for Depression Awareness, and the National Suicide Prevention Lifeline. She recently completed her first novel and enjoys fly fishing, kayaking, and dispelling the myth that you can't have your cake and eat it, too. For more information, please visit www.TerryWise.com.

Foreword

Life can be painful if you do it right. Anyone brave enough to love another person, anyone who loves enough to take onto herself another person's pain and fear, anyone compassionate enough to feel the pain of all that is wrong with our world, learns how challenging life can be. Sometimes the heart that opens itself to love becomes so overwhelmed with the feelings to which it has made itself vulnerable that it breaks.

Terry Wise's true story, told here in narrative form to streamline her experiences, is the story of a heart that broke from the pressure of too much love and too much pain, and of a brave therapist who was willing to open herself up in order to put that broken heart together again.

Terry is, of course, the central character of the book. We follow her descent into hell, the depression that followed her young husband's agonizing death, her wish to follow him into that oblivion where there is neither love nor pain, and her slow, faltering return to life and to a readiness to live and love again.

But Cali, Terry's therapist, is similarly heroic in the book. Though some of the names are invented, the dialogues between Terry and Dr. Cali Joseph have the ring of truth. I have known many therapists, personally and professionally, and I can appreciate how fortunate Terry was, at the lowest point of her life, to find herself in Dr. Joseph's care.

No one comes to see a therapist to tell them how happy they are. There was a time when therapists were expected to secrete themselves behind an emotional curtain and not let themselves become emotionally involved in the lives of their clients. After all, they deal with so many emotionally troubled people, all of them desperately needy. Fortunately,

Dr. Joseph chose not to abide by that rule. She dared to care. She dared to venture outside the box of standard clinical protocol, making herself available. Rather than simply presiding over Terry's voyage of self-discovery, she took Terry's hand and accompanied her on her journey.

What will you gain by reading *Waking Up*? You will read a gripping story. You will find yourself cheering for Terry with every tentative step she takes to return from death to life. But more than that, there are life lessons here for us all.

You will learn that heartbreak need not be a fatal condition; that a broken heart, like a broken leg, hurts terribly, but ultimately can heal. You will learn something about the incredible resiliency of the human heart and soul. There are people for whom the pain of life is just too much and they break under its impact. But there are people who can survive the worst that life can deal them. Sometimes the secret of their survival is an inner strength that they always had, but never knew they had. Sometimes it is a strength they borrow from someone else.

Waking Up is the story of a brave woman who dared to love and found that love left her abandoned in the valley of the shadow of death. And it is the story of a courageous therapist who dared to care about that woman, to lend her strength until she grew strong enough to continue on her own, to believe in her despite everything, until she learned to believe in herself, who took her by the hand and led her out of the shadows and into the sunlight. It is the story of a journey that teaches us how hope and a thirst for life can be restored. We will read this story and perhaps we too will be less afraid to love.

HAROLD S. KUSHNER, Natick, MA
Best-selling author of
When Bad Things Happen to Good People

Adorations

I spent an embarrassing amount of time debating whether or not to write a generic page of acknowledgements, which would run the risk of offending those who deserve specific mention, or to write an extensive, detailed list of names, which would run the risk of trivializing the profound contributions of so many. Lawyers can't make a decision. Trained to view every perspective, I find myself in a state of perpetual confusion, unable to move forward without factoring in every global consideration. Yet it wasn't until I sat down to write this page did I realize that that education in confusion didn't hold a candle to what two years of psychotherapy was going to do to me in terms of not being able to make a decision. So, I apologize in advance for any perceived oversights or diminished honors.

I have been blessed with an exceptional combination of friends and family who were kind enough to inspire me during the times I needed words of encouragement, and candid enough to slap me with brutal honesty when I needed re-direction. This book was written to capture the pivotal therapeutic moments that shifted my perspective from one of complete despair to one that is rich in hope and filled with the promise of an emotionally healthy, fulfilling future. However, the most important lessons I learned were gathered from the backstage support that doesn't get to take a bow during the performance. It is with these acknowledgements that I hope to lift the curtain and recognize the people who deserve to be front and center.

First, I would like to thank all those who inflated my ego when I was filled with rejection-induced self-loathing.

A difficult publishing process was made endurable with the lifelines that somehow learned to tolerate my incessant beliefs that "this time is different" and "maybe they are right," and doggedly remind me to stop focusing on the misguided.

To all my readers and critics who became a champion editorial team, whose input shaped each chapter with far more than red pen marks. Peg McNary, Fred Barron, Erin Liedel, Carolyn Bliss, Sande Kurland, Laura Zigman, Penny Donnenfeld, and Cathy Glaser. To Staciellen Heasley and Jill Cohen, who generously extended themselves, offering me much appreciated professional courtesies.

To my warehouse of treasured friends, particularly those who loved me enough to lie blatantly when I needed to believe that the road ahead would get easier, and to instill a faith that obstacles were just platforms from which I would spring forward. To Betsy and Scott K., Deb, Justin, Jo, Tim, Dan, Richie and Janice, Peter O., Wendy, and Bob H.; each one of you form a loop in my safety net of friendships.

To Erin (Given) Langton, who dared to voice the words and ease the pains that tormented me as I traveled down the ALS road of spousal care-giving; who showed me that the light at the end of the tunnel was the sun, not a freight train coming toward me.

To Verene and Tom, who transcended the conception of friendship, and occupied the space beside me in the foxholes of my battles and during the glory of my victories.

To my family, Steve, Connie, Alexa, Dad, Slim, Mom, Kellie, Shirley, Janice, Howard, and Betsy, who patiently stood by until I was ready to divulge the subject of this "mysterious" book, and who then managed to wrap their arms around me when I braved telling them that the opening chapter was indeed non-fiction.

To the people who influenced me in more profound ways than they ever could have imagined. Jeanne and Fred Barron, whose literary inspiration when I was 8 years old became the vein of my future. Ron Nicynski, who taught me everything I needed to know about sales and the people skills that would augment all of my future business endeavors. Peter d'Errico, who unburdened me with his insight that having a lot of questions was the sign of a multi-dimensional mind, not a limited one. Sarah Mathews, whose simply stated suggestion to add more dialogue spun this book in a new direction. Ali and Neysa, who despite the distance, will always remain close to my heart. Widy, whose soothing cologne and brief presence will forever provide a softened overlay to an otherwise tragic memory.

To the staff at Peet's® in Wellesley and Starbucks® in Wayland, who caringly poured thousands of cups of coffee while I tapped away for months at a time in my own world at the corner tables.

To Barry Farber, Judy Teplow, John Kalafat, Lyn Duncan, Lanny Berman, John Draper, Carol Wogrin, Dinelia Rosa, Arthur Dell Orto, the ALS Association, and DBSA, whose letters of endorsement have become a permanent presence on my Wall of Inspiration.

To Shonda Schilling, who sets the example of what it means to have a philanthropic heart and who confirmed that even the busiest of people can find the time to help others.

To Harold Kushner, whose endorsement provided me with the first day of pure joy I had experienced in almost seven years. The unbounded generosity of your time and your unwavering belief in me were central ingredients to the existence of this publication.

To Bob and Sue Levine, who were kind enough not to seek a restraining order against me. My thumb never hit the spacebar without the presence of your unconditional faith in me (and the fuel of a chocolate supply). It was your loving guidance that navigated the course I traveled to get here.

To Phyllis Parsons, a rare hybrid of literary agent, business manager, publicist, and friend. Not only did you surpass your goal to become a part of something meaningful, you amplified a message that has, and will continue to, save lives. Retirement? I don't think so.

To Michael Olson and Darren Kirby at PESI. I have no doubt you will exceed all expectations and get this book into the hands of people who haven't yet been touched by hope. Thank you for seeing its potential and for making both a business and personal investment in this journey.

To Chris, who restored my faith that I could indeed have another LOML. "You have the best natural ability to love that I've ever seen." The rest of the world will just have to cope. And how could I not thank Eric, Edes and Sarah? Each one of you has enriched my life in ways you have yet to learn. Chris, the competition continues, and I intend to win…Bingo. Forever.

To Betsy Glaser, who defines "generosity of spirit." Each page in this book is a dedication to your ability to make the seemingly impossible possible to resuscitate hope from an anesthetized soul. Every time someone gains an insight, expands a perspective, learns or even debates the lessons contained in these pages, every time this book inspires a life to be lived, or imparts a message of hope, it will be a tribute to the gifts you have given me. Thank you for shining a floodlight into the black hole and for teaching my feelings how to wear a new set of eyes. The real final lesson: Pinky promises shall never be broken. And, oh yes...nothing is random.

To Mr. Banichek, whose fate will provide me with a lifetime of laughter.

To Pete, whose offer to give me the tips of his ice cream cones said it all. Who etched a permanent smile in my heart with the memories of an eye roll toward the doctor, an "mmm" with the drip, a passing comment about the man in a wheelchair, the hoe, a reminder about deafness, messing up the drawer, and an unconventional request for Halloween. Thanks for the ride. We'll meet again, standing on the edge of the jetty.

DEDICATIONS

To Pete, for opening my eyes, in more ways than one.

To Betsy G., for becoming the yardstick
by which I will forever measure kindness.

To Chris, for paying the valet.

To the people who found the time.

Table of Contents

NOTE: The information contained within these pages is factual, but names have been changed to protect the privacy of those involved and minor modifications have been made to preserve the flow of the story.

Prologue

The Broken Promise

I'm not sure, but I think my husband committed suicide.

Christmas Day, 2000

On December 25th, just fifteen months later, I sat alone, cross-legged on our bed in the very spot I felt his last pulse. The day was going to become quite different than how I had customarily spent Christmas mornings. It was a day that now bears the distinction of my attempt to be the next in line.

With the tip of my left finger pressed on the cap, I used my right hand to spin the jug of morphine like a top. I stared at the black print of Kurt's name on the prescription label and the date it was filled—the day we were discharged from the hospital— a date that was as surreal as my current decision to take my own life before nightfall. This was not what the hospital pharmacy had in mind when they provided me with more than enough doses to keep Kurt comfortable.

"A, b, c, d, e, f, g, h," I had begun. I felt Kurt squeeze my hand when I got to the letter "h."

"H?" I asked.

"Yes," he signaled with a single, confirming squeeze.

"A, b, c, d, e, f, g, h, i, j, k, l, m, n, o," and another squeeze on "o."

"O?" I continued.

"Yes," he indicated again.

Muted by total paralysis, decoding the remainder of Kurt's words became the defining moment of our stay in the hospital.

"C-a-l-l h-o-s-p-i-c-e," Kurt spelled through eyes of pain.

I climbed onto the edge of the hospital bed and nuzzled up alongside of him. Kurt managed to turn his head my way, smiling his signature smile. I slid one hand beneath the collar of his hospital gown and the other through his hair, leaned over and kissed his forehead. Seeking a momentary escape, I paused to inhale his scent, hoping it would carry me on an excursion back to the shelter of healthier times. Yet, even the weight of my memory could not anchor me.

"Are you sure?" I quietly gasped, struggling to catch my breath.

The affirmation of Kurt's single squeeze lasted longer than the usual "one for yes, two for no" signal. Blood drained from my face.

We both knew what his refusal of nourishment would entail. Hospice would supply the morphine. It would be administered by me to quell hunger pains while we waited through an indeterminate period of days or weeks for starvation to take his life. "Call hospice" signified his decision to go home and die. Early the next morning, we drove out of the hospital parking lot to begin his descent.

"You are not the one killing him; Lou Gehrig's disease is killing him," the doctor volunteered days later, as I pumped another dose into Kurt's unconscious body. I refrained from voicing the retort about to spring from my tongue, "Call it

what you want, but it looks and feels to me like I'm helping him end his life." Instead, I kept silent and listened to the doctor's attempts to reassure me.

With authorization to increase the dosage, I hung up from the 3 A.M. telephone consult and returned to my bedside post. It was my job to prevent his pain, it was my job to respect his wishes, and it was my job to see him through the end of the four-year neurological battle we had been fighting. However, I did not realize at the time what was in store for me: Kurt would soon leave me alone on the "post-mortem battlefield" to continue waging the war without him.

Fifteen months after I watched him take his last breath under the dim lighting of our bedroom, I sat shadowed in the same light, defeated by the taunting reprieve of surrender.

I closed the book I had studied on assisted suicide and poured what remained of the morphine into a glass, wondering if I could speedily gulp down the thick syrup as instructed. The blue-colored liquid had not lost its menacing appearance since I last laid eyes upon it, just after the funeral more than one year earlier. We hadn't needed much to get through the five days it took for Kurt's suffering to come to an end. Caught up in the frenzy following the mortician's departure, no one thought to dispose of the leftover narcotics that filled my drawer—except me. His medication instantly transformed into my poison as I stored it away for later use.

I began another count: 60 doses of morphine, 200 Percocets and a large glass of gin. A plastic bag lay next to my pillow. As though sifting through sand, I lifted the pills into the cups of my hands and let them trickle through my fingers back into the pile on the bed. What was the correct amount? What was too much? Too little? Should I use the plastic bag?

My attention turned to the discovery I had made several weeks earlier at a deli. I am certain that everyone else in line was scanning the bakery items behind the counter in order to select what they wanted for breakfast. I, on the other hand, stood there, preoccupied with the dilemma of whether to live or die, noticing the optimal size of the plastic bags used by the store. I had even engaged in the ghastly practice of placing one of those bags over my head, not only to test its size and durability, but also to test whether I had the nerve to endure it. The "don't panic, just relax" suggestions in the book were terrifyingly impossible.

Aside from mustering up my distorted notion of courage, I recognized that the plastic bag method was complicated. In the event of a drug miscalculation, sealing it over my head before I went unconscious would ensure suffocation. It was a 100 percent surety that I would never again open my eyes. But, how could I mercilessly allow my family to discover me in a scene more fitting for a horror movie? The hideous sight of my lifeless face, shrink-wrapped inside a plastic bag, would be a permanent image replayed in their minds forever. I'm not sure which weighed on me the most—protecting them from the added trauma, or sparing myself from those few minutes desperately sucking against the plastic for oxygen. Ultimately, by not factoring in the bag, I decided to take the ten-percent chance that an overdose would fail.

This was not the first time I had gone through the procession of laying out the necessary accoutrements. However, this was the first time I had meticulously covered every last detail. I put my mail on hold, cleaned out the refrigerator and tidied up my closets. I prepaid all of my bills and made sure the "Do not resuscitate" directives of my health care proxy could be easily located. I wore the consoling fabric of Kurt's jeans and his favorite t-shirt that I had saved. There was a tranquil silence, the shades were drawn, and the overhead light was emitting a slight glow. My surroundings were virtually identical to the day of Kurt's death. In a peculiar way, I found the eeriness of the atmosphere more soothing than disconcerting.

I had become reclusive enough since the funeral to cover my absence with obscure references that I was going out of town for a few days. My need to get away from the difficult atmosphere of the holiday season was understandable. Everyone would be too distracted by their own holiday engagements to give a second thought to my whereabouts. All of the people in my life trusted me implicitly. My unforgivable betrayal was about to make fools of every single one of them.

Hours passed. Other than hypnotically twirling the plastic bag around my fingers and occasionally lifting up handfuls of pills to compulsively perform another recount, I did not make a move. It's strange to look back on what was going through my mind. One would think it was the sadness of saying good-bye or the anxiety of second-guessing my decision. It was neither. My thoughts, which were ordinarily too active for me to bear, vacillated between hosting an unfamiliar blankness and racing with unrelenting concerns. It was an adrenaline rush of clarity and catatonia in one—an inexplicable combination of emotionless fear.

I was preoccupied with the minutiae. My focus was largely on logistics and minimizing the aftermath. First, there were the purely selfish concerns. What recipe was the most lethal? Should I drink the entire jug of morphine and skip the Percocets? Should I crush the pills or just leave them in tablet form? Should I just go ahead and take everything, despite the risk of vomiting the fatal dose? The god damned plastic bag. How much was too much? How much was too little?

If I was doomed to wake up, what kind of brain damage would I sustain? Would I linger for years in a coma? Would I destroy other organs? Rivaling as one of my most acute fears was the terror of waking up in restraints, confined to a psychiatric ward. Would I lose my freedom and independence?

Although the nobility of selflessness was not a virtue I could include in my resumé, I struggled with the obsessive cycle of concerns about the impact on others. Would my therapist, Dr. Joseph, hold herself responsible for my actions? Would my family sue her? Should I write a note, imploring them not to hold her at fault? Would she despise me? I had promised her I would remain safe, that I would call her before I ever acted upon my desire to die, and she trusted me. There was no other way to interpret the statement I would be making. It was the ultimate "Fuck you."

Pathetically, one of my predominant concerns was to lessen the trauma to the people who would discover me. Unable to transport myself to the morgue, I could not figure out how this was avoidable. Who would notice I was not heard from in days? What conditions would I create if it took over one week for them to find my body? Who would enter the house first? What would they be feeling as they walked down the hallway and into the vestibule outside my bedroom? What would I have done to them once they caught the indelible, first glimpse of my motionless feet? Shamefully, I admit that in the end, my inclination to prioritize the feelings of others meant shit to me. All that really mattered was to finish the job and overcome my fear that I would wake up and live to be held accountable for my actions.

During the years I spent tortured in my solitary debate, I had skimmed through many books about suicide. The most poignant statement I ever read suggested that the very fact that I was standing there, reading a book about suicide, meant that I had not made a final decision to die. However, after living in the hell of over two decades of exhaustive contemplation, for the first time in my life, I stood on the threshold of death's door with the numbness of a firm resolve.

On Christmas day 2000, I didn't just peer over the edge of a rooftop. I jumped off, feet airborne with the cement blocks of depression shackled to my ankles. The final thing I recall was swallowing the last fistful of Percocets. I did not make an attempt to commit suicide. I killed myself.

CHAPTER 1

Avoiding God

October 1998

First floor. The lobby was populated with the Monday morning rush, silently jockeying for position. All eyes were transfixed on the numbers illuminating in descent above the steel doors. Still wavering, I turned around to head back towards the parking lot. As though their collective stares had speeded its arrival, the elevator's distinctive ding sounded, and the doors opened up for the next rotation. Ah, to hell with it. I herded into the box and took the ride up.

Second floor. Coming here was a good decision. There was no way out of my life, but I needed help. Third floor. Fourth floor. Each one another tantalizing opportunity to change my mind. Why did I come here? Talking wouldn't change a thing. Fifth floor. What was one hour? I could at least give it a try. I stepped off and let the doors shut behind me. I was a half-hour early for the appointment anyway—plenty of time to reconsider.

Dr. Cali Joseph, Ph.D., Licensed Psychologist, Suite 528. I took a seat in the reception area, filled with people respectfully averting each other's glances. The atmosphere in the waiting room of a therapy office somehow tends to make you feel like you're sitting there naked. I slouched down into the cushioned chair, and tilted my head back. Dr. Joseph would need the basic facts. Just start at the beginning. But when *was* the beginning?

I suppose I could always start with the telephone call that shattered my dreams for the future. I let my eyelids close and my thoughts drift behind them.

Three years earlier, I had sat down on our bed, with the phone ringing beneath my hand, and glanced out of the bedroom window. The four seasons of the year had offered us our own motion picture of the beauty of time. The wedding was just three weeks away. Three weeks too long.

I cheerfully answered, assuming it was Kurt on his way home from work. To my disappointment, it was Dr. Tella, the physician overseeing tests Kurt had been undergoing because of a slight slur in his speech. We had been assured that the cause was an allergy lining the inside of his throat. A simple pill once or twice a day and he would be fine. I was in a carefree mood, as neither of us had considered anything more serious. However, on the other end, was a messenger I tried to wish away for all the years to follow.

"So, are you gonna fix my boy?" I jokingly began. A deafening pause followed, much too noticeable to ignore.

"Well, we found some abnormalities," he replied.

Abnormalities? The flow of my blood changed course and accelerated to warp speeds, threatening to burst all the organs in its path.

"What do you mean?" I asked quietly from my suffocating chest.

"Well, I would like you both to come in tomorrow morning so we can discuss it." The stuff that nightmares are made of was pouring through the phone.

My thoughts were scrambling for a front and center position, with terror and worry neck in neck in the lead. I tried to swallow, but my tongue was stuck to the bottom of my mouth. I needed something to drink. I needed to move. I needed to go food shopping, and pick up the dry cleaning. My mind and body were waging a battle, and instead, I just sat there on the edge of the bed, frozen, staring blankly out the windows.

I had to keep my cool. I couldn't let Kurt see the panic in my eyes. I knew he would think I was making too much of it. I laid down on the bedroom floor, and pressed in the numbers to call my best friend, Rose.

"Hey, do you have a few minutes?" I asked. I pleaded with her to tell me there was nothing to worry about. We reviewed every possibility we could think of. Tumor? No, that had been ruled out. Brain damage? Unlikely. A high risk surgery because of the problem in his throat? Yes, that was it. Yet, neither of us could bring ourselves to admit that we were not convinced.

Just after sunrise the next morning, Kurt drove to our appointment. As always, we were early. We sat in the newly constructed, hospital lobby. As I turned my glance from the windows with the sky view of the bustling inner city traffic below, my fears began to unleash themselves as I looked around and realized that there were no other patients on the floor. It was quiet, the other chairs were empty, and there were no doctors in sight. This meeting had been called out of ordinary business hours.

Dr. Tella walked off the elevator and greeted us. We followed him to a small examining room just across from the vacant nurses' station, and he shut the door behind us. We sat on stools, in a triangle, facing each other. I felt like I needed

11

binoculars to see Kurt, as the few feet that separated us began to feel like miles.

Dr. Tella jumped right in. "We found some abnormalities in your tests. There is nerve damage and degeneration that is indicative of ALS." ALS, ALS, ALS, ALS, ALS. His words echoed through my skin. It was as though he had moved his lips, but hadn't said anything. It was a mistake. What about the throat surgery?

Kurt crossed his legs, reaching forward with both hands to grip his ankle, which was resting on top of his thigh. I had never seen him assume this nervous posture before. His body language started to shake me by the collar. He looked stupefied, trying to figure out what the object was that just struck him from behind.

Kurt squinted his eyes and asked, "You mean Lou Gehrig's Disease?" He sounded insulted, like he was saying, "You're wrong, and don't you talk to me that way."

Dr. Tella replied simply, "Yes."

Silence. In the span of 30 seconds, I had died and was immediately reborn into an entirely new body of indescribable agony. I would never see my former self again.

My hands and body were on the verge of noticeable trembling. Hysteria was rapidly swarming its way through me. But I managed to remain outwardly calm, and began my rapid interrogation. What are the chances you are wrong? How do you know the nerves are in the process of dying? It must be something else. And the clincher, "If it's not ALS, what else could it be?"

"There is NOTHING else it could be," Dr. Tella confirmed.

Nothing, Nothing, Nothing, Nothing, Nothing. Why was he still echoing?

"Maybe it could be a slower form of ALS that could take decades to progress," he added. Progress?! His alternative offered no consolation.

I stood up and managed to exhale a sound indicating that I had to go to the restroom. My body was moving towards the door, but I was no longer in it. I vaguely recall the doctor's mouth moving as he was telling me where the restroom was located. I had been blindfolded, spun around, and dropped into a maze as I stepped outside the examining room and let the door shut behind me.

I was trying to breathe, trying to slow the flow of blood pumping through my head, trying with all my might to resurface. Where was the rewind button that could get us back to the morning before, when we had our whole lives ahead of us? I splashed some water on my face and neck, pressed my hands against my face to rub out some of the paleness, and proceeded back to *the room*.

I walked around the floor looking for the door, but they were all the same color and shape. I felt like I was lost, looking for my car in a ten-story garage that was filled with cars of all the same make and color. The floor seemed so much emptier than when we had gone in. Somehow, I managed to locate the door, and re-entered the room with the composure that later became my namesake.

Kurt was standing. "How long do people with ALS live?" he asked.

"Two to five years from diagnosis," Dr. Tella straightforwardly replied.

We had to get out of there. There were no answers that would alleviate the oppressive thickness of the air. Dr. Tella gave us a couple of pamphlets on ALS support groups, and a referral to a neurologist who specialized in the disease. Speechless, with not so much as a glance at each other's face, we walked out the door.

Kurt stopped at the restroom, and I waited for him by the plate glass windows beside the elevator. I was always quiet and reserved. But I was no longer me. I leaned on a concrete column, and for the first time in my entire life, my reflexes put my skills of composure in a headlock, and flipped them upside down, knocking the wind right out of my body. I began to uncontrollably sob. Loud gasps emerged from a place so deep inside of me, a place that I had never been introduced to before. I openly wept without a care of who was around to hear me because, bodies or not, no one else was there.

Kurt came up behind me, gently reached out, and murmured, "Let's go." We walked, his hand resting on my shoulder, eyes to the floor, into an elevator full of people who now lived in the rest of the world.

We got into our car and just sat there in the darkness of the parking garage. Kurt didn't even reach to put the keys into the ignition. He hadn't made a noise—until that moment. With his head pressed down against the steering wheel, he squeezed out a series of moans. It was a guttural hysteria. I don't know how long we sat there. It didn't matter, because now there was no place in the world we could sit without the unwanted company of our new stalker.

Shortly after we arrived home, I entered into what would become one of many regretful agreements not to speak of ALS to anyone. Kurt had already managed to turn devastation into repudiation. The phone began ringing off the hook. Word had spread that we were going to the doctor. Family and friends were calling with a rather unsuspecting concern. Positive there had been a mistake, Kurt insisted that we not let anything leak out until after we consulted the specialist.

I agreed to a cover story. There was a small amount of nerve damage around his vocal chords. We had an appointment with a throat specialist in two weeks to treat it. Fearful that the condition of his throat would prevent him from sounding calm, I fielded all the calls. Self-control and the tone of my voice became imperative to delivering the scripted news.

Kurt was so confident that it was not ALS, and I never wanted to believe anything more. But, there was that one nagging question, "If it's not ALS, what else could it be?" *Nothing.* Years later, the consequences of keeping my end of the agreement to keep silent unfolded like a snowball into an avalanche.

The door opened, and I was startled back to the present. A man emerged, presumably another patient, and hurried past me toward the elevator. Dr. Joseph appeared in the doorframe.

"Terry Wise?" she asked with a smile as she walked toward me. Dr. Joseph extended a hand, and introduced herself. Still questioning my decision, I nervously followed her back inside.

The office was small, and dimly lit, with academic achievements and degrees decorating the wall. She sat down in a large, high back chair. I took a seat across from her, and waited for her cue on how to proceed.

"So, what brings you here?" Dr. Joseph said, beginning our first meeting.

The furthest thing from my mind was that, in years to come, this would be the very seat I would buckle into during a ride that would likely save my life.

CHAPTER 2

Grave Dimensions

April 1999

Weeks away from my 35th birthday, I drove into the handicapped space in front of the Youngerman Funeral Home and opened the side door of the van. Kurt remained strapped in as I held down the toggle switch for the mechanical ramp to drop to the ground. Once I heard the requisite clang of metal against the pavement and tested its stability with my body weight, I pressed the big red button on the dashboard. The lock box on the passenger side floor clicked open and unfastened Kurt's powered wheelchair. Seeking the comfort offered by touching the warmth of his skin, I tucked my hand into the back neckline of his t-shirt as we proceeded quietly across the parking lot to make the arrangements.

Several days earlier, I had spoken to the owner, a family acquaintance, to explain the purpose of our visit. Rather than delegate the task to one of his staff, Stan Youngerman had decided to personally attend to our appointment. After a brief greeting, we were led to a small, windowless office in the back of the building. Kurt powered his way over to my side.

"What kind of funeral do you want?" Stan began with a stuttered opening directed at Kurt. Meeting with the deceased was a rarity in his business.

Clearly unnerved, Stan's eyes darted furtively around the room. Seeking the solace of a familiar habit, I began to twist my wedding band. Only Kurt appeared at ease with planning his own funeral.

I'm not sure whose idea it was originally, but somehow, we had come to the conclusion that it would be unburdening if I had one less responsibility to manage after Kurt's death. Looking back, it seems a rather remarkable notion.

ALS, more commonly known as Lou Gehrig's disease, had taken its course. Kurt's mind remained unaffected and trapped inside the progressive paralysis of his body, his tongue virtually immobile. What remained of his speech were now unintelligible tones, requiring me to act as his interpreter. His condition left me with little choice. Consequently, I accompanied him to a meeting that I would have otherwise found inconceivable to attend. Fielding traumatic appointments had become routine for us over the past several years. Thus, I had developed a proficiency at being present in body form only and had little fear of passing out right there on the floor.

We began with the obituary. The first part of the decisions was relatively straightforward. Did Kurt want it published in the major newspaper alone or in conjunction with the local community papers? Did he want his photograph next to the wording? Did he want his cause of death to be named? What relatives did he want to list? How do you spell their names and how are they related? Stan completed the form and read the abbreviated, standard obituary back to us for approval. It was kept simple.

Stan's trembling fingers caught my eye, and my attention momentarily diverted to the near bloodless grip he had on his pen. I could almost see the flow of tension rushing to his fingertips and wondered if the strain of appearing undaunted would cause him to inadvertently crush the pen into a spray of ink. Strangled with poise, he resumed his questioning.

Do you want an open casket for a family viewing before the funeral? A religious wrap of some kind or your own clothes? Who do you want for pallbearers? We were bombarded with choices. What do you want your stone to say? Do you want it placed on your grave immediately or postponed for a formalized unveiling ceremony? Where were people going to offer condolences? How many folding chairs would be needed at the house? He even presented a couple of oversized boards that had "kits" stapled onto them to display the variety of candles, thank you cards, sign-in books and black ribbons.

"What type of casket do you want?"

Stan had moved on to the question I most dreaded. I had been lying awake for months trying to prepare for the anguish of burying Kurt alone in that airless box. Despite my stoic demeanor, I experienced an onslaught of opposing feelings crashing around my body like emotional bumper cars.

"Would you like to go to the display room and look at a few of our floor models?" Stan continued sheepishly.

Contrary to the years, I had indomitably weathered the ravages of ALS on Kurt, perusing the empty caskets was a feat I was certain I couldn't face without vomiting. Thankfully, Kurt immediately declined the tour. As preposterous as it sounds, I was relieved when Stan produced a catalog of 8x10 photographs of caskets with varying dimensions.

I was opposed to having a funeral. To ensure that I would be cremated, I had even made specific provisions in my will. No gathering. No ceremony. No memorial. No costs. Kurt disagreed with my beliefs. Candid discussions did not dissuade him. He believed in the comfort offered by grieving together rather than apart. As always, I obliged his requests.

The choice of caskets was vast. Prices ranged from the more economical pine box to the very costly solid mahogany with all the bells and whistles. After briefly weighing the price of each model and its specifications, the selection was made. I slowly pushed the coffin catalog back across the desk towards Stan. We were finished. Or, so I thought. Instead, the one question that caused Kurt to lose his composure followed.

"How many State Troopers will be needed? The average is two, but I suggest at least four in order to manage the traffic and direct the funeral procession," Stan delicately explained. Obviously, his familiarity with Kurt led him to believe there would be a large number of people in attendance. The air was thick with tension, as I sat through an interminable silence awaiting Kurt's response.

"None," Kurt retorted dismissively. "They won't be needed." I interpreted his answer for Stan.

Stan anxiously looked to me for a supportive confirmation. I felt Kurt's hand start to sweat in mine, his forehead beaded with perspiration. The disease had weakened the muscles in his chest and the reflexes that controlled his expressions, and the exaggerated frown that contorted his face made its irrepressible appearance. Difficulty breathing was sure to follow. I reached over and patted his forehead dry. Gripping his hand more firmly in mine, I looked into his eyes and reluctantly, with a very gentle smile, gave a slight nod of agreement.

I realized my Achilles heel that day was and always will be his casket. However, it took me a long while before I understood why that particular question about the police escorts evoked such pain for Kurt.

Kurt had lived a full life, rich in relationships. People were important to him and played an enormously significant role in how he chose to spend the bulk of his time. He had maintained a wide range of relationships that developed from each period of his life, and the companionship of family and friends was at the heart of his existence.

Kurt refused to allow his diagnosis to sabotage what remained of his life, and instead, strived to live with a passion for the moment. While insulated by the comfort of this enthusiasm, his philosophy required a disconnection from the path of his illness. Thus, the planning of his funeral had become somewhat isolated from the web of his relationships. Stan's question blindsided him and stripped off his cloak of detachment. The number of people who were going to be affected by his death became a startling reality.

Stan was right. Six months later, there was standing room only at Kurt's funeral.

CHAPTER 3

Uncommon Courtesy

October 1998

"So, what brings you here?" Dr. Joseph said, beginning our first meeting.

"I've been under a lot of stress, and a friend of mine recommended you."

"Then I'm glad you called. How can I be useful?" she asked.

"I'm not sure. I saw a therapist for a short time, a year or two ago, but it didn't work out," I answered, still fighting the urge to run back to my car. Forty-eight minutes remained on the clock.

"Why do you think it didn't work out?"

"Well, I didn't need a place to go just to unburden myself. I know there are a lot of people who benefit from the confidentiality, and the ability to vent to someone who won't pass judgment. In some ways, maybe that's helpful for me, too. But, what I really needed was productive *interaction*. I didn't want a head nodder," I explained.

"What do you mean?"

"I wound up doing ninety-percent of the talking. He would just sit there, furiously taking notes like dictation, nodding his head, and saying, 'hmmm' about ten thousand times."

"How long did you see him for?"

"I don't know, maybe a few weeks. He also had a rather unorthodox philosophy. He said that he had an 'ethical issue' with the insurance industry, and therefore, didn't accept *any* medical insurance payments. I had to pay cash, up front, before every appointment. He wouldn't even accept a personal check."

"Wow. That's incredible. I've never heard of anyone doing that before," Dr. Joseph replied disbelievingly.

"I should've just left, but I tried to stick it out, hoping that a more balanced dialogue would develop. But, instead, he seemed to absorb sounds like a human tape recorder. I don't ever recall getting any meaningful feedback from him. There wasn't one time when I drove off feeling any sense of relief," I explained, still feeling the exasperation of his silence. "But, then again, I'm not sure if I'm really cut out for counseling. It seems I've missed whatever it was designed to offer. Or maybe there's no feedback that I would ever find helpful, anyway," I hopelessly continued.

"What were you trying to get relief from?"

"It was after my husband, Kurt, was diagnosed with ALS," I said. Since the very first time I uttered the words, they had never lost their sting.

"I'm sorry to hear that," Dr. Joseph responded softly. My first impression was that she was a little too sickeningly sweet for my liking. Later, I learned that I had never been so wrong. It was a caring sweetness that partnered with a hard-line tenacity, but it was never in a sickening way.

"Yeah, I was sorry to hear it, too. Are you familiar with the disease?"

"Yes, a little bit. But, why don't you tell me more?"

I embarked on my standard explanation of Kurt's condition. We had received the news that he had Lou Gehrig's disease two years earlier. It was causing progressive paralysis throughout his body. His mind would never be affected. It was typically fatal within two to five years of diagnosis, and therefore, the exact amount of time he had left to live was indeterminable. There was no treatment. There was no cure. We were still newlyweds.

"How long were you married before you found out he was sick?" she asked.

"Well, actually, we were told three weeks *before* our wedding," I replied.

"Gee, what incredible timing. I want to ask you again how I can be most helpful to you. It sounds like things must be really tough."

"That's the thing. I *don't know* how you can help. I have a hundred emotions to deal with every single day, and none of them are very good," I reluctantly answered, hesitant to complain.

"Well, why don't you just start with one of them?"

I deliberated between the most pervasive feelings of pain, guilt and resentment for a few moments. "Resentment," I chose.

"What do you feel resentful about?"

"A million things. It's overwhelming to think about everything at once."

"Again, let's just take things one at a time. Just pick anything you feel resentful about," Dr. Joseph suggested, helping me get past the difficulty of sorting it out.

"I just want to have a normal life again—like it was. I can't bear to watch Kurt getting worse. I want all the heartache to stop, and to have *my life* back. I want him to have *his life* back." Tears filled my eyes.

"That sounds unbearable, Terry. How long have you known Kurt?"

"About six years."

"Do you have any children?"

"No. I suppose we could have tried after the wedding, but it's hard to think about starting a family when your husband has been given a death sentence," I cynically replied, shocked by my own bluntness.

"Of course," Dr. Joseph kindly responded.

"I mean, no one ever knows how long they have to live, but I think it's safe to assume that most other couples enjoy their honeymoon without having to cope with a black cloud of death. It's so hard because, when other people get married, they get to celebrate a beginning, not prepare for an end. I never got to have that blissful optimism about our future," I explained, tears now streaming down my face.

"It's perfectly understandable that you would feel resentful about that, Terry. You are 34 years old. You were denied something that most people get to enjoy without a second thought," Dr. Joseph sympathized.

"Yeah. For those three weeks before our wedding, I had to go through an excruciating number of champagne toasts, photographs, and lots of smiling. Then, I had to come home from my honeymoon, feigning the overjoyed newlywed. No matter where I went, I was thrust into environments where my demeanor was constantly on display in the spotlight. Kurt virtually required me to pretend like nothing terrible was happening. People kept congratulating us, and asking about our plans for the future. I felt like shouting in their faces, 'The only thing I plan to do is find a way to return our wedding gift of Lou Gehrig's Disease.'" I could feel the revival of my resentment.

"So why didn't you just tell people that it was painful, and to stop asking?"

"Because no one knew."

"*What do you mean?*" Dr. Joseph squinted.

"No one knew," I repeated, affirming her dismay. "For a long time, Kurt refused to believe he had ALS. So, initially, I promised not to tell anyone until he could prove that the doctors were wrong. We told immediate family and close friends that it was 'probable ALS,' but the tests weren't conclusive, yet. Technically, it wasn't dishonest because, there is no diagnostic test for ALS.

"That's one of the other fringe benefits of the disease," I added sarcastically. "The only way to diagnose it is to eliminate all other possibilities—tumors, stroke, and so on—and then wait it out to see what happens. There's a test that analyzes if the nerves in different parts of your body are dying. It's not considered a "firm" diagnosis until three limb areas begin to show nerve degeneration."

"That sounds awful. How long did you have to wait until you knew for sure?"

"I *did* know for sure. Kurt's speech was getting worse, we were seeing ALS specialists, and they told us there was *nothing* else it could be. But Kurt was very obstinate. Even when they told him definitively that it was ALS, he then refused to believe it would be fatal."

"How difficult that must have been," Dr. Joseph responded, careful not to interrupt the flow.

"Yeah, it has been a series of relentless conflicts. Sometimes I would find myself wishing for a conclusive diagnosis, just so part of the anticipation would be over. But, then again, that hellish limbo kept some hope alive. It was a no-win situation—wanting to know, and *not* wanting to know at the same exact time."

"You must have been very confused."

"Yeah, you can say that again. I mean, it looks like ALS, it sounds like ALS, Kurt was under the care of an ALS neurologist, and I was interpreting for him because his speech was steadily deteriorating. But, I had to live as though it wasn't a reality. Truthfully, there was a part of me that was hanging onto a thread of hope that Kurt was right, and that it was some sort of cruel, marital test. But, as the list of ALS-in-my-face tasks engulfed me, it became undeniable—to me, anyway."

"You said that Kurt 'required' you to pretend?"

"Yes. That just compounded the confusion and resentment. On one hand, it has been great for Kurt to have such a positive outlook. In fact, even through today, he manages to be happy with each day of his life. I don't know how he does it. He's in a wheelchair, he can't bathe, eat, dress or speak for himself. But, somehow, he has maintained an emotional constitution that refuses to waste even one moment feeling down. It's terrible that I feel this way."

"I don't understand. Why are your feelings terrible?"

"Because, *Kurt* is the one who is sick, *not* me. And, I want to spare him the torment. I *want* him to be hopeful, and maximize all the time he has left with as much happiness as possible. But honestly, in some ways, his outlook has made things even worse for me."

"How so?"

"Because, I'm under constant pressure to keep up the façade. Even when I saw that therapist, I had to conceal my appointments because Kurt considered it a waste of time to suffer over an illness he didn't have. Since there was nothing to worry about, grief had to stop and we had to renew our excitement for planning our future. And even though it was patently obvious that his condition was deteriorating, I had to live in a world that was looking the other way. It was the proverbial elephant in the room. Everyone walked around it, as though it wasn't there."

"What do you mean? What did people do?"

"Initially, everyone followed Kurt's lead. So no one talked about it, no one cried about it—or if they did, they did it privately. But, of course, I also understand that people wanted him to remain hopeful. And, naturally, they needed to feed off of his hope for themselves. Besides, if *he* was capable of being happy, then of course, *no one else* was going to fall to the floor in despair."

"What would've happened if you joined Kurt in the way he was dealing with things?"

"It would've been impossible. It *is* impossible. I interpret for him full-time. I feed, shower and shave him every day. I sleep next to him and feel his body twitching all night. I even left my job so I could help him run his business. So, as strange as it sounds, I've never had the luxury of denial, because *I've* had to deal with it *every single day*."

"That doesn't sound strange to me at all. I can see why you feel resentful," Dr. Joseph stated.

"Having the rest of the world walk around smiling all the time is very alienating. No one talks about it. No one *has ever* talked about it," I stressed in a tone of disbelief. "Everyone comments on how commendable it is for Kurt to have such a positive outlook. And I agree. I would certainly hate having to deal with the alternative. Who knows, maybe no one has talked to me about their pain because they think they're making it easier for me to deal with it—just like I think my silence is making it easier for Kurt to deal with it. But I would so much rather have *someone* acknowledge the fucking horror of it all. Regardless of what the reasons for the silence have been, our worlds have separated. And, the place Kurt lives only has room for one of us. I can't afford to look the other way."

"You mean, *Kurt and everyone else* can't afford to have you look the other way," Dr. Joseph suggested.

"I don't want to think about things that way, and I don't want to be angry. Everyone is doing the best they can. I know they care and wish they could do more to help. But, that's the other thing. Kurt doesn't want anyone else doing things for him. The bottom line is that being resentful is not helpful to me at all. I don't know, Dr. Joseph, I never have one consistent emotion. Everything I feel is in perpetual conflict."

"You don't have to call me 'doctor.' Most people call me Cali. Whatever you're most comfortable with."

"Okay," I replied, appreciating the offer.

"I would really like to talk to you more about this. But, we have to end now. Can we make another appointment?"

"Yeah, sure," I answered, taking a shocking glance at my watch. I had gone from counting the minutes until I could make a run for it, to losing all track of time.

"I'm looking forward to hearing more," Dr. Joseph said, as she stood up.

I wasn't sold on therapy just yet, but there was something intriguing about talking to her, and a different light had been shined on the experience. At that point, I would have been willing to explore a voodoo-based ceremony if it offered any hope for alleviating even a small portion of my anguish. Whatever the reasons, I was pleasantly surprised to discover that a part of me wasn't ready to leave.

CHAPTER 4

The Route of the Question

November 1998

I continued to meet with Dr. Joseph over the next several weeks. I filled her in on my relationship with Kurt, and the emotional pandemonium that erupted after his diagnosis. Feeling the most profound contentment of my life had devolved into the pain of losing more of him with each day.

Although I continued to stubbornly refute the relevancy of my past, and confine our discussions to the present conditions of my life, at a minimum, Dr. Joseph's office provided me with one precious hour of freedom per week. It was a place where I could just sit without the angst of having to take care of anyone else, and unclothe from the uniform of my composed appearances.

"What is a nervous breakdown?" I began one day, as I took a seat.

"What do you think it is?" Dr. Joseph responded.

Given my overall propensity for immediate gratification, I was irritated that she would rarely just answer a question.

"I don't know. That's why I'm asking," I repeated.

"But I would like to know what *you* think a nervous breakdown is," Dr. Joseph pushed back.

"I don't know," I argued, growing increasingly frustrated with her unwillingness to answer me.

"Well, what do you think would happen if you had one?" Dr. Joseph urged.

"*I don't know*. Do *you* think I could have one?"

"If you don't know, then just take a guess. I won't hold you to it."

It hadn't occurred to me that I could attempt an answer unless I felt my thoughts were accurate. Eager to gain insight into my current beliefs, Dr. Joseph was going to force me to struggle through a response, rather than provide me with the less helpful spoon-fed reply. I was too worn down to maintain my usual obstinacy. It was obvious that she was not going to back down, and I just wanted to move on.

"I think a nervous breakdown is when something catastrophic happens, or you are so flooded with stress or trauma, that you start rocking in the corner, unable to recognize anyone," I answered, feeling the crushing weight of my sorrows beginning to mount.

"Have you ever seen anyone that you thought was having a nervous breakdown?" Dr. Joseph cleverly tried to dig a little deeper.

"No," I replied, with my more truthful answer tucked behind the wall of places that were off limits.

"What about when you were growing up?"

"That doesn't matter, Cali," I protested. "Anything I'm feeling today has nothing to do with my childhood. The past is the past. I already understand that part of my life completely, and I don't need to talk to you about it." For weeks, I had been consistently resistant to her probing.

"I disagree, but okay. I want to respect your feelings about it." Dr. Joseph's hands were tied. Our relationship had not matured enough for her to become more assertive. Anything beyond a slight push and she knew I would be out the door.

"Tell me what is happening *now* that makes you bring this up."

"I'm just so exhausted, Cali. I cannot afford to become non-functional. I have to be there for Kurt," I explained, hoping for her assurance that I was going to keep my wits about me.

"What could happen that would make you non-functional?" she persisted.

"If my mind just snapped, if I lost touch with reality, and then became unable to fulfill my responsibilities."

"What are your responsibilities?"

"It's too complicated to explain. I don't know. I can't separate the things I do all day. Everything is just a part of everything, and it would take too long for me to explain," I answered.

"Can you tell me about one thing that is exhausting you?" Cali was forced to make adjustments to her therapeutic approach, but she continued to find any way in that she could.

"Wow, this is pathetic. I don't even know what to choose," I replied, overwhelmed by the list that was compiling in my head. "I suppose eating is a good example. Kurt can't lift his arms, or use his fingers anymore. His tongue is completely paralyzed, and he chokes constantly," I explained. "Eating is a major production. Everything has to be prepared so it's really soft. He can't move his lips anymore either, so even taking a drink is very time consuming." I despairingly thought back to an appointment the week before our wedding, when the doctor taught me how to perform the Heimlich maneuver on my fiancé. We all smiled and shrugged it off as precautionary. But the daily hazard of choking to death had caused a new form of tension to immediately inhabit my body. I never relaxed during a meal again.

"No one else feeds him?"

"No. Sometimes, I have to stick my fingers in his mouth to help move the food around. It takes an inordinate amount of time and patience to get through each meal."

"What do people with ALS do if they can't swallow their food?" Cali asked.

"They get feeding tubes. Keeping weight on is a huge issue for people with ALS. They can't afford to lose any body fat, because they lose muscle along with it. It's a constant battle to keep enough nutrition and calories going into him," I explained, thinking about the fatigue of the daily routine, and how many meals I had missed as a result of the angst and the work that it took to feed him.

"So, why doesn't Kurt get a feeding tube?"

"Because, Kurt *loves* food so much that he's willing to take the risk of choking to death. He really shouldn't be eating anymore. The doctors have already warned him about the hazards, including aspirating food into his lungs—which would not be good, because it would cause pneumonia. Lots of people with ALS die from pneumonia because their breathing is too weak to fight it. But, you know, it's easy for everyone else to say, 'oh, just go get a feeding tube,' but that stinks. That really stinks."

"But, wouldn't it be a lot easier *and* a lot safer?"

"Yeah, but it's his call. Kurt is very stubborn. He wants what he wants, and I don't want to take things away from him that he enjoys. It's kind of an ass-backwards world. We're always looking for high calorie, high fat things he can still eat. My sister-in-law is a chef, and she's been trying to find softer meals that taste good. I try to make him the things he loves. Ice cream goes down better than most things, so I make him a lot of sundaes and milk shakes every day. Plus, he has piles of pills that I have to lay out for him to take three times a day, and the only way to get them down is with ice cream or pudding." I paused, feeling the exhaustion of it all.

"Terry, do you realize that other 34 year-old wives don't have to do these things for their husbands?" Cali asked, staring at me incredulously.

"Yeah." Surely I knew that it was far from the norm.

"No, I don't think you understand what it looks like from the outside of your life anymore," she suggested.

"I know how it looks. But, I am physically capable of helping him to eat," I replied from the securely fastened straightjacket of my life. "Kurt still resists allowing anyone else to help him with his care. I know most of it is because of his pride, and I'm trying to preserve as much of his dignity as possible. He can't even shower or use the bathroom by himself anymore. I'm not squeamish about that kind of stuff. It's hard enough on him as it is," I explained.

"How long have you been doing all of this?"

"Well, it has come in stages. He started to have trouble with his index fingers about two years ago. So, shaving and helping him shower started around that time. I guess I've been doing more and more since then."

"So, let me get this straight, Terry. You are the only one doing those things for him every day?"

"Yeah. I don't want to deprive him of the things he had before. He loves to be showered and shaved every day, and I want him to feel good," I replied. "I know what you're thinking. But I'm strong enough to transfer him in and out of his wheelchair."

I immediately regretted uttering the word 'transfer.' I had always strived to remain considerate, and whenever possible, minimize the indignities of Kurt's dependency. 'Transfer' had become 'move,' 'feeding him' had become 'helping him to eat.' Although I felt a twinge of guilt for momentarily abandoning that sensitivity, I found it relieving to have the ability to relax, if only for *an instant*, about something—even if it was just my choice of words.

"You lift him by yourself?"

"Yeah. I have a system worked out so that I can get him dressed, or in and out of the bathroom or our bed."

"What do you do during the night?"

"Well, neither one of us gets much sleep anymore. His legs cramp and he has to be turned a lot. I know other people who sleep in separate rooms, and hire someone to help out during the night. But, he's lost so much already, and he always talks about how lucky he is not to have to give up sleeping together. There's *no way* I could make him lie there with someone else in the room. He's awake too much and it would be hell for him to feel like someone was babysitting him. I am fully capable of doing all of these things."

"So, you take care of him, plus work all day, and then you're up for most of the night?"

"Yeah, but I can do it."

"Oh Terry, just because you can physically do these things does not mean that you can do them psychologically."

Cali's words hit me like a bolt of lightening. I was treating fatigue like a nuisance, not an obstacle. I knew I had become desensitized to many of the adjustments I had unconsciously made during the slow progression of Kurt's illness. But my mind hadn't snapped, and I wasn't rocking in a corner. My hands worked, so I could shave him. My mouth worked, so I could speak for him. My legs worked, so I could bring him the things he needed.

"Of course you are capable of doing everything. But needing a break is not insensitive, and it has *nothing* to do with your physical capacities. You need to get some help with his care, Terry," Cali insisted.

Time was fostering an inverse relationship between our needs. As Kurt's condition required more of me, my strength and stamina were steadily declining. But as long as I was still standing, any notion of refusing to help him had been inexcusable to me—until now.

"I know the potential affect on my mind. I guess that's why I'm worried about having a nervous breakdown. But, it's hard to deny him whatever dignity he has left. I simply cannot force him do anything he doesn't feel comfortable doing. I can't imagine if it was me, and someone else made the choice about who would take care of me."

"I understand. But, Terry, have you thought about the choices *Kurt* is making?" she asked, with another striking blow to my perspective.

"He didn't choose to be sick," I retorted defensively.

"I understand that, but what are the choices he is making *for you*?" Cali said, continuing to hammer away.

"Well, I know he is choosing to have me as the only one who takes care of him. But a lot of his needs are really personal. Imagine if you were completely paralyzed, and had no choice over who was going to put your bra on, or take your pants down and sit you on the toilet. I just can't do it to him." Despite the personal consequences, guilt had a stranglehold on me.

"Doesn't that make you angry?" Cali attempted to elbow my conscience out of the way of my own good.

"Yes, but it's at the situation, not at Kurt."

"I realize that Kurt didn't ask to be sick. However, *given the situation*, what would *you* require of him?"

I didn't want to see her point, but there it was. It was another direct hit that shoved me across the threshold of the door to a new understanding. I almost didn't have to answer.

"I wouldn't have the same expectations of him," I confessed. Like it or not, the metamorphosis of my thoughts was in full momentum. "No, if it was me, I would feel *horrible* about having him do anything for me. Especially, if he was *this* exhausted."

"Terry, you need to take care of yourself. I'm not suggesting that you be angry, but you need to have a talk with Kurt. It's time for you to get some help."

Over the course of the following weeks, Dr. Joseph's follow-up inquiries encouraged me to begin elaborating on the specific conditions of my current life. The side in favor of my own well-being started to win out, and I began to recognize some of my human limitations. She helped guide me through terribly difficult conversations with Kurt, and adjusting his expectations of me. As a result, I was able to enlist the help of others for some of his care.

It took me several years to understand why she delayed answering my question about a nervous breakdown. In order not to cut off a valuable part of the process, Dr. Joseph always insisted on dissecting any question first. It was an inroad to opening me up, and enabled us to explore a maze of underlying feelings that wouldn't have been apparent had she just immediately answered me. I learned that the process of getting to the answer was just as important as the end result. Cali never assumed anything. Clarifying *why* I was asking was just as important as knowing *what* I was asking. Even though I believed my reasons were obvious, I often didn't understand how critical it was to know what was behind the question.

I wouldn't budge on my refusal to discuss my childhood, and how it may have impacted my present feelings. Dr. Joseph could only work with what I gave her. But, she adapted to those limitations, and continued to target more concrete ways I could improve my current life. Certainly, we could not change the past, and much of the present was going to remain unyielding, but we were still able to make progress working around the parameters I had set. Even if nothing else came of our meetings, she was intent on instilling the belief in me that I had a right to take care of myself. I had a million justifications

41

for bottling up any notions of self-interest. But they would no longer withstand my new awareness.

Our talks continued for several more months, but as Kurt's condition declined, I ultimately chose to leave therapy. Despite her conviction that she could help me further, continuing to talk about it was only making me even more aware of the unfairness and brutal realities of my life. Each week we met, I found it increasingly difficult to return to my life at home. Things were only going to get worse, and I knew that I would need every bit of strength I had to manage what lay ahead. Regretfully, I was too clouded to see how I could have benefited from remaining in treatment. However, the seeds for our future relationship were planted. We had only spoken for a few months, but the process had unknowingly begun.

CHAPTER 5

The Yin-Yang of Flowers

September 1999

There are many things to consider when you are planning a family event. Among a litany of other considerations, you must think about the list of people who will be attending and the atmosphere you would like to create. As I walked down the stairs after delivering Kurt's eulogy, I was unavoidably permeated with the scent of fresh flowers. It was then that I realized the distinct difference between choosing flowers for your wedding and choosing them for your own funeral.

I had spent the last hour evading even the slightest glance toward Kurt's now occupied casket on the stand in front of me. The culmination of assaults from the previous few weeks was pummeling me. I had not gotten more than a couple of hours of sleep per night for as long back as I could remember. I was malnourished, weakened by extreme fatigue and impaired to the point of intoxication. Nevertheless, I began to feel slight relief from reaching my goal to remain conscious during the eulogy. I took my seat in the first row. Eyes to the floor, all I could think about were the flowers.

The beauty of mind travel rescued me from the remaining portion of the service. As the funeral resumed, my mind drifted out the door of the Youngerman Funeral Home back to the spring of 1996.

Kurt and I had decided to be married in Newport, Rhode Island, a place that was special to us for a number of reasons. We had taken a drive there for the day in order to choose the date and the exact place where we would get married. We decided to exchange our vows outside, at the edge of the water. We chose a spot on the sprawling lawns of a park with panoramic views overlooking the ocean. Afterwards, we went to lunch to begin listing the people and things we wanted to have present.

I was in favor of keeping our wedding simple. If it had been left up to me, there would have been no planning. We would have purchased a couple of simple wedding bands, driven down to Newport ourselves and sought out a Justice of the Peace. Our vows would have been exchanged at the side of the ocean, wearing jeans and sweatshirts. The wedding celebration dinner would have consisted of loaded nachos, steaks, and cold, dark beers.

As we began to reverse the stereotypical roles during pre-marital discords, Kurt would have no part of it. He wanted a wedding. He wanted the tux, the dress, the photographer and the expanded guest list. We worked out a compromise over a shared shrimp cocktail and a couple of glasses of champagne. Simplicity with a handful of guests would do.

Then there were the flowers. Kurt and I both loved fresh cut flowers. However, I had not even considered them until Kurt mentioned it. Buying them for just one day didn't feel worth it to me. There would only be a few guests to offer them to and the rest would all be thrown away after we checked out of the inn where we would stay overnight. Kurt insisted. He didn't care if we had the flowers for one hour. He felt that the creation of a certain atmosphere far outweighed the cost or length of time we would enjoy them.

Kurt located a nearby florist. I sat back in amusement
as he ordered dozens of the most fragrant, gorgeous flower
assortments. They were blended with white tulips and
daisies—my favorites. He made arrangements to have the
flowers delivered to the room several hours before our arrival.
He wanted the entire place to be full of aroma.

I learned a valuable lesson on the day before our wedding.
As we carried our bags through the door, my heart filled
with warmth as I breathed in the powerful scent of Kurt's
thoughtfulness.

The funeral director's voice startled me as the names of four
friends, chosen as pallbearers, were called out and asked to
come forward. My mind crashed as it landed back in my front
row seat. I couldn't bring myself to look up at Kurt's casket as
it was carried by. I stood up to follow the trail of shoes worn
by those four young men, with the congregation of mourners
behind me. As I walked out the door of the Youngerman
Funeral Home into the most gloriously perfect, sunny fall day,
Stan's questions flooded my mind. Flowers or no flowers?
How much do you want to spend? Flowers draped on your
casket or just to the side? What kind of flowers? I found myself
climbing into the car behind the hearse, wishing more than
anything that we had chosen white tulips and daisies.

CHAPTER 6

The Trip

November 1999

I opened my eyes to the unfocused view of the white, marble countertop of my kitchen center island. Dazedly lifting my head, I felt the flat markings on my cheek—fossilized lines from the stacks of condolence cards that had served as my unforgiving pillow. The rays of morning daylight blowtorched through the windows, stinging my eyes like a spray of fire. A candle was still burning—flickering light off the plastic prescription bottle and the adjacent martini glass, which had been left standing with a toothpick full of olives. I glanced down to my bare feet protruding from torn, blue jeans. Fully dressed, once again, I had made a bedroom out of the kitchen barstool. Any attempt to categorize it as falling asleep would have been like depicting a coma as dozing off.

I knew I would be depressed after Kurt's death. Yet, progressing through the grieving process had become a fiction. What had begun as an occasional evening of temperately anesthetizing myself had deteriorated into a routine of teasing death's door with a potentially lethal combination of prescription drugs and alcohol. Excessiveness had swallowed up moderation, and the notion of "just taking the edge off" had become a thing of the past. In the two months following the funeral, I had created a world of Russian roulette where my survival had become based upon the pure luck of passing out just short of an overdose.

The consequences of being a 35-year-old widow appeared to be the rather obvious cause of my despondency. ALS had left me in the aftermath of its tornado—a vortex that seemingly passed over everyone else's home, but picked mine up and spun it through space for four years. Dreadfully, I discovered that there was no Oz in sight.

I gathered up the debris around me, and began a day that, predictably, was about to become a repetition of yesterday. As I placed the envelopes back neatly on my desk, I glanced over at the sheet of paper I had unfolded and left in view. Dr. Joseph's unexpected, handwritten note of condolence, which had arrived three weeks earlier, had never joined the pile of post-funeral sympathies. Singled out for later consideration, I hadn't spent much time entertaining her kind offer to remain available to me.

I was losing the daily battle against the insatiable appetite of depression, and each time I washed down another sedative with the gulp of a martini, the monster of hopelessness took another huge bite out of me. The appealing notion of suicide was perched on the forefront of my mind, blinding my eyes from the possibility of a tolerable future. Although I had no intention of relinquishing my private world of chemical retreat, somehow, through the haze, a barely audible voice hidden deep inside emerged with enough strength for me to recognize that I needed help.

The usefulness of my meetings with Dr. Joseph months earlier still resonated. The note on my desk was just the reminder I needed to reconsider grabbing onto the life preserver she had penned and mailed my way. I had already spoken to friends and family about the weight of my sadness over losing Kurt. I still wasn't sure what more I could learn, or what could be gained, by reiterating any of it to a therapist. After all, our talks would be about knowing me. It was my mind, my memories, and my life. I was convinced I knew all the issues, that I was stuck with the memories of recent events, and that my childhood was irrelevant.

However, the insights we had gained during our previous work offered me some hope that talking with her again might be relieving—even if I was still intent on confining our discussions to the present. Despite my continuing skepticism, I somehow arrived at the decision to call Dr. Joseph and schedule an appointment.

I walked back through her door with a few nagging questions I had yet to put into words. I knew I was being vaporized. My life had gone from a non-stop sprint to a screeching halt. But why was I still exhausted? Why was I declining into emotional inertia? Why were things still deteriorating all around me? Why was I intent on destroying myself? I knew that I could not sustain my life much longer without the answers.

"It's so confusing," I began. "It feels like Kurt was given a death sentence, and now, I've been given a life sentence. I can't seem to maintain one consistent emotion, and everything I feel is peaking simultaneously. The confusion I felt when Kurt was alive pales in comparison to this."

"Why is that confusing to you?" Cali asked.

"Because, I can't reconcile how I'm feeling. I feel terribly guilty that there is *any* relief associated with his death. But then I agonize over how much I miss him. Then again, the *relief* isn't relief in the traditional sense. It's not what you would feel if you thought you had a brain tumor, and then the tests came back that you were healthy. It's almost like the definition of "relief" will never be the same for me. Because feeling it means not having Kurt," I explained, generating yet another layer of confusion. I found it strangely alleviating to articulate my feelings about the concept, as I had not spoken of them to anyone before. However, *any* form of reprieve still felt impermissible to me.

"Don't you think that it's possible to have all of these emotions at the same time?"

"Yes, but that's what is making me so miserable," I replied. "I hate how I feel."

"I can understand that. But hating your feelings doesn't make them go away."

"Well, then I'm really screwed. How am I supposed to deal with feeling all of this?" I asked.

"You learn how to face things. You talk about what you are feeling so that you can sort them out, and understand them. I'm not saying that talking will make the feelings disappear. But, your understanding of them will change and therefore, they will grow to have less power over your life," Cali explained.

"But I've had plenty of time to prepare for Kurt's death, and I can't seem to pull it together," I hopelessly replied.

"Terry, why are you so hard on yourself? It's only been *two months* since Kurt died. Two months," Cali said, raising her two fingers in front of me as she spoke. "Some people can't even get out of bed for a year after they lose a spouse. Please, give yourself a break."

I didn't understand how I could justify feeling so terrible, so torn, so tired, for this long after Kurt's death. Two months seemed like an eternity to me.

"I'm still so exhausted, Cali. I can't seem to re-acclimate my body to a normal routine," I said, purposefully omitting my nightly submersions. "It's been so long since I've eaten my meals without tension, or slept for more than a couple of hours at a time."

"Did you ever get any help caring for Kurt during the night?"

"No," I replied.

Months earlier, Dr. Joseph had tried to persuade me to get assistance for overnight stays. I had forgotten she wasn't privy to the caregiving decisions that were made during the last few months of Kurt's life. In spite of the obvious consequences of sleep deprivation, I had chosen to stay with him every night.

"It was my choice," I continued. "But Kurt ended up coming around towards the last few months, and I know he would have accepted it if I had decided otherwise. I'm paying the price for it now, but I do not regret my choice. Besides, it's *one* less thing to feel guilty about." Images of Kurt, unable to simply turn himself over, were tearing at my heart. The flip side of my exhaustion ached to be next to him again. I hadn't slept in our bedroom since he was carried out the door. "Your words were very helpful to me," I said.

"Which words?" Cali asked, surprising me with the question, missing an important opportunity to dissect the guilt I had just mentioned.

"That even if I could do everything physically, it didn't mean I could do it psychologically. It was a real eye opener, and it helped me make a lot of other changes before he died." Died. Even though I had watched Kurt take his last breath on our bed, my mind could not absorb the language that was now sliding off my tongue.

"I'm glad that our work together was helpful. I know it was difficult for you," Cali softly recalled. "What were some of the changes you were able to make?"

"It took a while, but in the last few months of Kurt's life, I was able to ask others for some help, and Kurt was able to accept that I couldn't do it all."

"It sounds like some things did get better, even though Kurt was getting worse," Cali responded, acknowledging the paradox.

"Yeah. You know what's even stranger? For almost four years, the indeterminacy of when Kurt was going to die was maddening. I always thought, 'If I could just know *when*,' but then when I knew, I *didn't* want to know. It's so insane in here. I'm a walking contradiction," I said, pointing to my temple.

"*And*, since the moment I first heard the words 'Lou Gehrig's disease,' I was desperate to stop time, and plug up the hourglass that was turned over on us. But there was also a part of me that yearned to see the end of the anguished road we were on. However, now that I find myself standing on the edge of its pavement, the only thing I want to do is drive off of it," I said, with my first real hint at the depths of my depression.

"Has your family been supportive?" Cali asked, relentlessly looking for an opening into my past.

"Yeah. But, all the relationships are very complicated, and I don't want to get into any of that right now. If I start thinking about everything in my life, I'll become one of those people who doesn't get out of bed for a year," I said, sarcastically referencing Cali's "two month" warning.

Dr. Joseph leaned forward, as though she were looking through my eyes, reading what was inside of me. "Terry, during the months that we've known each other, you have always demanded that the past remain in the past," she began with a soft directness. "But, if you want to figure these feelings out, and feel better, you are going to have to deal with how your earlier experiences might be influencing the present. In spite of what you wish, you cannot separate periods of time."

I shook my head, immediately balking at the notion that my childhood had anything to do with the current way I was feeling. I was the poster child for the concept of randomness, and consistently rejected anything that resembled a standard textbook theory as generic psychobabble.

"When you are ready, Terry, I can take you there," Cali said quietly, her eyes still locked onto mine.

Something immediately stirred inside of me. To my astonishment, this seemingly inconsequential remark triggered a feeling that I hadn't experienced before. Perhaps it was Dr. Joseph's choice of words, her demeanor, or the timing. Or, maybe it was feeling the warmth that I could be "taken" to undiscovered places and cared for. Maybe it was a combination of everything.

Although I was already traveling on my own self-destructive journey, I stepped out of Dr. Joseph's office that day with the first ambivalence about where I was headed.

Something had baited the monster of hopelessness, and intrigued me about the mind trips we could take within her four walls.

CHAPTER 7

Leap of Faith

December 1999

Still damp from greeting another kitchen sunrise drenched in painkillers, I took a seat in Dr. Joseph's office. My baseball cap pulled down low over my eyes, I languished in another hangover masqueraded as exhaustion.

Dr. Joseph continued to chip away at my protests that the past was not an integral factor in understanding the present. However, even to me, it became increasingly evident that we were trimming the top of a rapidly growing weed, rather than looking below, and pulling it out by its roots. As my indifference to life became more apparent, it was clear that the time had come for us to take a step forward in the process. But first we had to start with trust.

"Have you ever thought about suicide?" Dr. Joseph asked, wasting no time.

Shocked by the directness of her question, I paused to catch my breath. I had asked for brutally honest interaction, not hand-held tempering—and I got it. I wondered if she could see the brightly lit letters of my answer, "Y-e-s, it's-all-I-think-about," scrolling in a banner across my eyes.

"I don't want to answer," I replied, struggling in the debate between honoring my commitment to honesty and my fear of ever answering that question truthfully again.

"Why don't you want to answer?" Cali asked.

Fifteen years later, I would still hear the keys rattling outside my door. I would never chance going back there again. But how was I going to risk telling her the truth? How was I going to risk *not* telling her the truth? It was inconceivable to me that anyone was capable of hearing my feelings without a panic-stricken response.

"Play it out, Terry. What would happen if you told me?"

Every word was lodged in my throat. I didn't even know how to work up the courage to tell her why I *wasn't* telling her. Unwavering in her pursuit, Cali never broke her stare. I considered throwing her a bone, so we could just move on. But, I already knew that refusing to answer because of fear would be an invitation for her to unceasingly persist.

"I was hospitalized when I was in college. It was a complete waste of time, and I will *never* let it happen again—*never*," I declared.

"Why were you hospitalized?" Cali continued.

"I would rather not say."

"Why not?" she persisted.

"I don't know," I shrugged my shoulders, eyes to the floor. Dehydration was fueling my anxiety.

"I don't know is not good enough. Why won't you tell me?"

"Because, I just *don't* want to talk about it. It's not a big deal anyway, Cali," I protested.

"If it's not a big deal, then it should be no problem to tell me about it."

"I can't," I said, squirming in obvious discomfort.

"Was it a big deal to *you*?"

"Yes," I murmured.

"So, don't you think it would be helpful if you told me more about this part of your life?"

"I don't think so." I paused for a moment. "Yeah," I finally agreed, rolling my eyes in surrender.

"So, why were you hospitalized when you were in college?"

"Okay," I sighed. "I agree it might be helpful for you to know. But, I *really* don't want to talk about it right now," I stubbornly replied, biding time.

"Tell me why. I'm reasonable, Terry. I won't push you, just for the sake of talking about something. If there's no purpose to it, or you can explain reasons that make sense, then we'll move on."

That seemed fair enough. But the drill to an inevitable answer was starting to become more familiar. I had a choice between answering, and then talking about it, or *not* answering, and then going through the painstaking process of explaining why I *didn't* want to talk about it. Either way, it *was* going to get tabled.

A dozen reasons raced through my mind, but I couldn't come up with anything other than the terror of winding up back on that ward.

"I was hospitalized because I told someone how I was really feeling—that I wanted to die," I said, braving the answer. "I'm *never* going back to a hospital," I repeated.

"What makes you think that would happen here?" It appeared that the visor of my cap had concealed the banner scrolling across my eyes.

"Because that's what happened the last time I was completely honest with someone about how I was feeling."

"Who were you honest with?"

"A therapist I saw during college." The cushion below me began to transform into a block of cement. Supporting myself for an imminent collapse, I sat motionless, with my feet planted firmly on the floor.

"Are you okay?" Cali paused, noticing what she assumed was my standard "anxiety stance."

"Yeah," I guessed, struggling to conceal my nausea.

"You look pale. Are you sure?"

"Yeah. I'm anxious and I didn't sleep well, but I'm fine." Lightheaded from the previous night's liquid escape, I hadn't yet included omitting the details in the definition of dishonesty.

"Okay," she said. My cover of fatigue worked. "Did you try to kill yourself when you were in college?" Cali resumed.

"No," I answered, not volunteering another syllable.

"Did you have a plan?"

"I don't know," I hesitated.

"You don't know?"

"I can't say."

"Why? Is there something wrong with your throat?"

"No. My throat is fine," I replied, feeling both trapped and challenged. Even if the exchange continued for weeks, I knew Cali would keep the issue alive until she found a way in.

"Yes, I had a plan. Well, it was more like an idea. I had some sleeping pills, but I never came seriously close to acting on it. I don't even think I had enough of them, anyway," I finally answered.

"So, how did you end up in the hospital?" she asked curiously.

"I'd rather not say."

"Why not?"

"Because, I just don't. I know this sounds paranoid, but I'm afraid of telling you why I *don't* want to tell you," I admitted.

"Well, try to play it out. What do you fantasize would happen if you told me?"

"I'm not sure," I fearfully answered. Words were filling my mouth with the temptation to tell her, but my fears locked them in like gated racehorses. I had promised myself that I would never fall prey to the illusory safety of anyone's confidences again.

"What would happen? Play it out," Cali persisted.

"All right." I took a deep breath. "The reason I don't want to tell you is because, the therapist I was seeing took me by surprise. If I tell you, I'm afraid you'll learn from what happened before. If I ever feel close to suicide again, I'm afraid you would come up with a different plan to lure me into your office. So, I'd wind up hesitating to ever tell you the truth, and you would wind up hesitating to believe me whenever I tried to assure you I was safe," I explained, as my words were released from behind the gate. I knew I could only keep my life going for so long if I didn't start trusting her.

"Well, that sounds like a difficult dilemma for you so, let's just take it one step at a time. What do you imagine happening if you told me you were suicidal? Would we be talking on the telephone? Would you come into the office?"

"I don't know."

"Well, just think about it," Cali waited.

I had to know if Dr. Joseph would ever deceive me. A number of entrapment scenarios raced through my mind. As I thought about her questions, I began to feel slightly less threatened by her respectful pace, and the realization that she sincerely wanted me to trust her. She didn't seem to be gathering information for the purpose of sending me to a hospital like the other therapist had done. My paranoia about a set-up began to ease. It was time to take a leap of faith.

"I had spoken to my therapist on the phone about how depressed I was feeling," I began. "He asked me if I was suicidal and I told him the truth—that yes, I was. He asked if I would come in to talk with him. I felt relieved to get an immediate appointment. When I arrived, he asked me more questions. 'Have you thought of a plan?' 'What is your plan?' I answered truthfully. He then informed me that my mother was in the next room. In the time it took for me to get to his office, he had contacted her, and the hospital." Completely airborne, I paused, swallowing my fear that I had leaped too far. "It became clear that I was either going to agree to sign myself in, or I was going to be admitted involuntarily. So, I agreed, and my mother drove me there. It was completely useless, and I've *always* regretted telling him the real truth about what I was feeling."

"How did you feel when you left his office?" Cali asked.

"I was shocked and afraid. Even though I absolutely disagreed with his decision, I believed, at the time, it was because he cared about me," I answered, churning inside about his betrayal.

"So, you trusted him, and ended up in a psychiatric ward?"

"Yeah. It was a bad time."

"Do you think I would ever call someone in your family? Or that I would ever do that to you?"

"I don't know. It's not the calling of someone I fear nearly as much as the decision to have me hospitalized," I proceeded. "Believe me, it would *not* be helpful. Maybe there are benefits for other people because deep inside, they want to be saved. But, that would *not* be the case for me. I would bide my time until I got out, and I would *never* trust anyone again, including you. I'm just not going to let you do that to me," I said emphatically.

"Terry, I wouldn't *do* anything *to* you. I would only do things *for you*," Cali responded. "Things have changed over the years. I'm not a huge fan of hospitalization. Unfortunately, there is a rush to discharge people. Even if I fought to have you admitted, you would probably be out soon afterwards. However, I *do* believe that it can be useful, if it prevents you from killing yourself. I would do *anything* I could to save your life, even at the expense of knowing you might never trust me again," Dr. Joseph emphasized. "Have you ever taken any anti-depressant medication? Would you consider it now?" she continued.

"No. I've never been on any meds and I absolutely won't take them. Honestly Cali, unless you could promise me that you would *never* force me to go to a hospital, I don't think I could tell you any more about how I'm feeling," I admitted.

"I don't understand why you're so adamantly opposed to medication. But, we can talk about that later. If things were to ever get that bad for you again, I *cannot* promise that hospitalization wouldn't be a consideration. But Terry, *I can promise you* that I will work as hard as possible to explore every other option first," Cali attempted to reassure me.

"Like what?" I asked, intrigued by the possibilities. I *wanted* to trust her. Although not optimistic about a resolution, I found myself hoping that she could pave the way for me to talk more openly to her about my feelings.

"You could call a friend, or family member, and ask someone to come stay with you. Or, *I* could call someone for you. You could take medication. You could promise to have me paged, and give me the chance to talk to you on the phone. Or, we could try to meet. I can't promise I will always be available to you, but if you called and told me you needed to talk, I would do everything I could to make the time as soon as possible."

The alternatives Dr. Joseph presented weren't nearly as comforting as a firm promise from her, but anything short of involuntary hospitalization was certainly a welcomed consideration. The mere fact that she was even willing to try so hard to find ways in which to help me began to ease more of my fears.

"We have to trust each other, Terry. I *can* promise you that I will *always* talk to you first, and try to work out something other than hospitalization. And if anything changes, we will discuss it again, and again, and again. I have complete faith in our ability to work *anything* out. I'm not interested in covering my ass. This process is about *you*, not about me. All I can work with is the value of your word. Can you give me a promise, in return, that you will call me first?"

"Okay," I whispered, hardly able to believe the sound that came out of my mouth.

I wasn't sure which side of the room was more worn out, but *my* stamina was certainly down to its reserves. I was exhausted, yet exhilarated. The first piece of armor around my black and white dogma, that a compromise about hospitalization was impossible, had been removed. Neither of us got everything we wanted, but I had taken my very first step into the new territory of a middle ground. Despite an unimaginable conclusion, we had reached an agreement that provided us both with the comfort of moving forward.

Although a long way away from fearlessly speaking my mind, a pocket of my soul had been unzipped. I was drawn to the glimmer of hope that perhaps I didn't have to live alone forever with the weight of my feelings. Less shielded, I found myself surprisingly relieved that full protection might not always be necessary.

I was still in the embryonic stages of understanding how the therapeutic process worked. However, in months to come, this experience ultimately formed the basis for instilling hope in me that anything could be worked out, as long as we continued to talk.

CHAPTER 8

Nixon

January 2000

"What don't you want to talk about?"

The backs of my legs hadn't even hit the seat, yet. Any sooner, and Dr. Joseph's question would've been asked while I was still coming off the elevator. Armed with the freedom provided by our agreement about hospitalization, she eagerly dove into her first round of in-depth inquisitions.

"I don't know. A bunch of things," I answered, stunned by her assertiveness.

"Well, name three of them," she continued.

"Hospitalization, my childhood, or *anything* more about Kurt," I replied without hesitation.

"Which one do you *least* want to talk about?"

"My childhood," I honestly answered.

"Okay. Let's start there," she replied, without missing a beat.

"Very cute, Cali," I sighed, slowly shaking my head. I should have known better than to assume she would go easy on me. Unsuspecting of her motivation, I had walked right into it.

"I know you don't want to talk about the past, Terry. But, I know so little about your history."

"What's to know?" I resisted.

"Well, for one thing, I don't know much about you as a little girl. I know you were depressed in college, but nothing before then. What were things like for you growing up?" she asked.

"I lived with my mother and stepfather. And, I was terribly shy," I replied, with the barest possible answer.

"Can you tell me about . . . . .," Cali began, but I could not hear her. I had begun to daydream myself right out of the conversation.

"I didn't hear you, Cali. I'm sorry. I just lost my focus," I explained, my anxiety on the rise.

"What's up, Terry? What did you just start thinking about?" she softly asked.

"I don't know. A few things, I guess." My thoughts felt like they were being hit around the inside of a pinball machine. I fought to concentrate on her words.

"Like what?"

"I don't know," I repeated, scrambling to avoid the route on which my thoughts had already taken me. "Anyway, it's irrelevant. Believe me, it had nothing to do with what we were just talking about," I replied, unable to stop myself from thinking about the one thing that kept coming to mind.

"O.K., so it's irrelevant. I want you to tell me anyway," she insisted.

"I mean it, Cali. I just started to zone out. It wasn't related to anything you were saying."

"That's fine. But, I still want you to tell me." Cali didn't let up for a moment.

"Alright, alright," I whined. I could hardly bear the strain of remaining focused, and my ability to protest was fading. "I was just thinking about President Nixon's resignation speech," I blurted out.

"Hmmm. That's interesting, Terry," Cali seemed surprised, with her head slightly cocked to the side. "What were . . . ."

There it was again. Her lips were moving, but I did not hear the sounds.

"I'm sorry, Cali. I can't stay focused. What did you say?" I asked.

"Wow. Something is happening. Where did you go?" Cali seemed genuinely intrigued.

"I don't know. What were you saying before I zoned?" I stubbornly asked again.

"No, Terry. I want you to tell me what distracted you. What is making it so difficult for you to pay attention?" Cali tenaciously persisted.

The more I tried to hide my anxiety, the more it heightened.

"I just started daydreaming. I don't know. Whatever I started thinking about had nothing to do with what we were talking about beforehand. Why won't you just *tell me* what you were about to say?" I protested.

"So, it was just a 'random thought'?" Cali asked.

"Yeah, definitely."

"Alright, it was random. But, I still want to know where your mind went." This is when I first learned that doing battle with Cali over who would answer first was a no-win situation for me. She was not going to backtrack until I responded.

"My mind just wandered. It's difficult to answer without getting into everything," I said, unable to distinguish my thoughts enough to explain.

"Well, let's try to take things one at a time. What was happening in your life when Nixon resigned?" Cali prodded. "It would be interesting to know what our conversation triggered in your unconscious."

"What do you mean my *unconscious*? I hate that psychobabble. Cali, it's very straightforward, and there is nothing more to understand here." Cali's look prompted me to continue.

"O.K., if you *really* think it's *that* important." I reluctantly readied myself to answer. "I remember going into my parents' bedroom to hold one of those old tape recorders up against the television speakers so I could tape Nixon's entire resignation speech. I was about 10 years old. Obviously, it was a big news event, and being so young, I thought it would be a valuable thing to have on tape," I partially answered, stopping short at the threshold of the door to places I desperately wanted to avoid.

"Who else was there during the speech?" Cali asked.

"My stepfather, Louis, was there. He was in bed," I answered.

"Where was your mother?"

"I don't remember. Probably downstairs in the kitchen or something. I don't know what made me think of it—it just popped into my head when we were talking," I said, barely able to convince myself of the coincidence.

"Where were *you* in the bedroom?" Cali asked, dismissing my attempt to sidestep the full picture.

"On the floor right next to the bed, I think." My mouth turned drier with each step closer to reviving the memory.

"Do you remember anything else that was happening at the time?"

"I don't know. I think it was the day that things started to happen with Louis," I responded, surprising myself with my own candor.

"What things?" she asked.

"It's hard to remember. I used to lie down with him a lot, and he always gave me backrubs. I was probably next to him on the bed." I paused for a few moments, hoping for an end to the conversation. But, suspecting there was more, Cali's expression asked me the next question. She waited patiently for me to continue.

"I think it was the first time he put his hand down my pants and started touching me." A wave of nausea rippled throughout my body. I had never spoken in this kind of detail to anyone before.

"Was anyone else in the bedroom?" Cali proceeded.

"No. I don't remember. I'm almost positive it was just the

two of us." Guilt and shame swept over me as though I were seated in a confessional.

"You said it was the first time. Were there other times?" Cali kept digging.

"Yeah. It happened a lot after that day. I don't know. Maybe it happened before that day, too. I can't remember exactly. I just know the places where we were."

"Where else did this happen?" Cali asked.

"Mostly in the living room. There were other places, too, but the majority of the times, I was laying with him on his easy chair, while he watched television."

"Did anyone else know he was abusing you?"

"It *wasn't* abuse. I've read all about it, and not one book has ever discussed what happened to me."

"What do you mean?" Cali asked.

"I've never read one story that talked about my situation. Louis did not use physical force. He wasn't threatening me, and I wasn't afraid he would hurt me if I refused. He was my stepfather for over a decade, and like it or not, I even used to call him Dad," I answered, recalling my years of turmoil over balancing the adults' names. "I am not going to play the victim. I am *not* going to hide my responsibility behind some common excuse," I adamantly explained, self-convicted.

"Do you think any of it was *his* responsibility?"

"Sure, it was his fault, too. Believe me Cali, I'm *not* excusing him from *anything*. I know he was a sick bastard. But, that doesn't mean *I* have impunity."

"Do you think any of it was your mother's fault?" Cali asked. In spite of knowing how much I detested the notion of anything that resembled the "tell me about your mother" approach, Cali was marching forward. Even if I didn't respond, she was going to send me home with a stream of new thoughts to contemplate.

"No. She didn't know what was happening. Besides, her priorities were all messed up back then. She couldn't leave because she was so dependent upon him—emotionally and financially. That is why *I've* worked so hard to be independent in my life. So, I don't blame her for what he was doing to me."

"Where was your mother when you were on the easy chair with him?" Cali continued.

"Usually in the kitchen, making dinner." I thought back to the smell of fresh food cooking one door away.

"Don't you think she has some responsibility, for not protecting you from him?"

"Sometimes. Partly. But, not in the way that you think. She definitely didn't know what was happening to me," I reiterated. "*But*, it was because of *her* choices that I was exposed to him. She minimized a lot of the unscrupulous things he did to her, and to other people. So, there were plenty of other reasons why she should have kept him away from me."

"If you could divide up the responsibility between you and Louis, what would you say are the percentages?" Cali asked.

"I don't know. Probably 20% him and 80% me," I replied.

"So, your mother has zero responsibility?"

Holding her accountable for any part of it felt like such a cop out for me. I had to think. The numbers seemed so arbitrary. "Alright. Well, probably 17% him, 3% her, and 80% me," I guessed.

"How old were you, Terry?" Cali asked. I anticipated where she was going, but it didn't matter. I knew the part I had played.

"I think it started when I was 10, but maybe younger. I can't remember the exact dates, but I can remember the approximate year by which house we were living in at the time and the trips we took together." I suddenly felt so confused. I was repulsed by the memory of him, while at the same time I felt a longing to be back there, packing my clothes with unbridled excitement for our Florida vacation.

"How old was he?" she asked.

"I can't remember. Probably a few years older than my mother." I didn't remember the year he was born, but I hated the fact that I had never forgotten his birthday.

"Terry, you were a child. He was an adult."

"I know. But, it's not like it was happening at the kitchen table with everyone in sight. So obviously, even though I was a child, I knew enough to know that it was wrong," I explained. I had had this conversation with myself a million times over the previous 25 years and always came to the same conclusion. There were no reasons, only excuses.

"Terry, you can't look at this in a vacuum. There are a million other factors to consider. You need to create a context. I realize it is impossible to remember every one of the facts, but that is unnecessary. We can recreate so much of your life at that time by understanding more about your environment. If you talk about it, you will know it and be able to understand it better," Cali proposed.

"I already know everything there is to know. I lived it. I understand it. I am *not* going to dwell on my past, or cop out with a victim-of-child-abuse claim. I *know* the context," I retorted, feeling the knots wrench tighter in my stomach as I recalled the *real* context—as *only* I knew it. Cali was not going to be able to understand what I was saying unless I divulged the *one* distinguishing factor that truly condemned me, but I could not get the words out of my mouth. I was hoping to make my point without it.

"Terry, you are remembering things *today* with an *adult* mind. You are viewing your childhood with the incorporation of a *lifetime* of experiences, and what you *now* feel is right or wrong. Your mind was different when you were a child. If we work on recreating the context, we'll have a better understanding of what you knew and felt *at that time*," Cali urged.

It was difficult to conceptualize what Dr. Joseph was saying. At that point, I believed that developing a context meant reaching into irrelevant, extraneous factors in order to find an excuse to let myself off the hook.

"But, I *do* remember, and it was *not* abuse," I continued to refute. "During the few times I've talked in general about what happened with Louis, what he did has been referred to as abuse. But Cali, there has *never* been *one* time when someone said the word 'abuse' without my feeling like a fraud. I've always gone along with the depiction—even though I've never really believed it."

"But, did you ever try to develop or understand the context, by talking it through, with any of those people?"

"No. I've never wanted to use what happened with Louis to get any attention, so I've always avoided talking about it," I explained. Although I felt ashamed of this "character flaw," I was surprised at how liberating it felt to tell her these beliefs about myself. I had never disclosed my fears about attention getting, or perpetuating a fraud to anyone. In months to come, I would learn how my fears of getting attention had unnecessarily silenced me for years.

"You don't understand, Cali. I *know* the real truth, and it's beyond the traditional 'child feeling at fault syndrome.' There is a lot more to it than what is described in the psych books," I continued.

"Terry, there is nothing you can't tell me. *Nothing*. I want you to be able to talk to me about anything. What more is there to it?" she reassuringly asked.

"I can't say," I replied. In all those years, I couldn't even bring myself to say it to the mirror. I knew that once I spoke the words, I would never again be able to go along with the perception that I had been victimized. Even though I did not feel abused, I had still been able to hold onto feeling a slight reprieve from concealing the entire truth. It was a reality I could barely live with myself.

"How can I make it easier for you to talk to me about it?" Cali asked.

"I don't know. I just can't say it." I knew that I needed to tell Cali everything. I knew it would be the only way she would understand the extent of my culpability. Actually saying it was an altogether different matter.

Dr. Joseph and I spent the next several weeks going over and over the information I had already divulged. But, the most important piece remained trapped behind my fears. I spent many nights sitting alone on my bedroom floor, trying to say the words out loud in the darkness of the night.

I didn't completely put it together at the time, but I gradually realized how critical it was to the very foundation of our work that Dr. Joseph knew the real truth about me. If I withheld anything from her, I would always have second-guessed her opinions. She needed to have all the facts before she could offer me insights that I would be able to trust, because I had to know she was basing her thoughts on the "true me," *not* who I held myself out to be.

After several more sessions, I finally worked up the courage to tell Dr. Joseph the one thing that had haunted me for years. Telling her was the most honest I had ever been with anyone—including myself.

"It wasn't abuse, because I knew it was wrong. I didn't have the strength to stop it . . . . *because it felt good,*" I whispered with my eyes to the floor. *There it was*—the one factor that no one knew.

"Terry, just because your body responded doesn't mean you were at fault. It is a natural, physiological response. You were at an age when your body was just waking up to sexual feelings, and that does *not* condemn you," Cali explained.

"Yes, it does. I wasn't forced to do anything. It's not like he grabbed me or physically held me down," I said, as I began to think about the new concept of what it meant for my body to start waking up.

Several moments passed as I began to wonder what it would have been like if I had my first sexual experiences with a boyfriend, rather than with Louis. Conversations I had with my girlfriends while I was growing up flooded my mind. I remembered how we used to sit around together and compare stories about what it was like to get to second base, third base, or any base for that matter. I always pretended to be on the same playing field as the rest of the girls. But, I had to lie. I spoke of my experiences with the boys as though they were my first introductions to sexuality. However, the truth was that I was very different from my friends. I already knew all about how it felt. Louis had taken care of that. He had denied me the normal progression of adolescent firsts.

"Oh, Terry. There are so many ways to force children to do things. Threats often come in very subtle forms. You have to consider the entire context," Cali insisted.

"Well, what do you think the percentage of my responsibility was?" I asked. It was very rare for Cali to answer, but this time she adamantly responded.

Cali looked me in the eyes and held up her hand in the "O" position as she unequivocally stated, "Absolutely zero."

"If you thought I was responsible, would you actually be able to tell me?" I asked. I was stunned. How could she not hold me at least partly responsible?

"Yes, I would. Terry, I promised you that I would never lie to you. I wouldn't say it if I didn't believe it. But, what I think is not the important thing here. It is what you think," she replied.

I hadn't the slightest idea where Cali was going. I had just revealed the most damning news about myself, and she was still insisting that I was not at fault. It took me some time before I realized how the process was already in motion. In the meantime, we continued to go in the direction she was pointing.

"Where were both of you when these backrubs were happening?" Cali asked.

"Mostly in the living room, while he was watching the Merv Griffin show every afternoon, before dinner," I answered.

"Did he call you to come over to him?"

"No, *I* walked over to him. *I* walked *over* to him," I repeated emphatically.

"What would you say? What would he say?"

"Nothing, I think. I can't remember anything being said."

"But, would you agree that it was likely something was said, or some gesture was made?" Cali asked.

"Yeah, I suppose," I replied. I knew she had to be right. I had never thought about the preceding moments in that kind of detail before. There had not been one crack in my ironclad self-conviction—until the following moments. The context was taking form.

"Well, since you can't remember what was said, then how do you know he didn't tell you to come over? How do you know he didn't whisper something to you that brought you to him?" Suddenly, I realized that I could not remember all the specifics. I didn't know if I was remembering what happened, or if I was remembering what I thought happened.

"Because, it couldn't have happened that way, Cali," I said, still uncomfortable with the notion of conceding to an "excuse."

"Why is it that if you don't remember what happened, you fill in the blanks with the assumption that you were the one who did something wrong? If you are guessing at what happened, why do you choose facts that are against yourself? Couldn't you just as well assume that he did or said something during those moments that you cannot remember now?" Cali asked.

I was literally speechless. There was no denying it: I had been so afraid of making excuses that I clearly overcompensated by clothing myself in almost complete responsibility. There was no way to refute her point. The crack began to widen. I didn't even attempt to respond.

"How old were you when all of this began?" Cali was relentless. She was going to backtrack until all the details I could remember were flushed out.

"I think it started when I was 10—or a few years before that," I answered, fully aware of Cali's implication. As an attorney, I completely understood the concepts of coercion, or lack of capacity as a minor. However, my memory of fearless cooperation still felt clear enough to deny me any of those defenses.

"How old was Louis?" she asked again.

"I don't know."

"Well, let's figure it out," she insisted. After some quick calculations, she came up with the estimation of mid-to-late 30s. "Terry, there were so many disparities—in age and in size. You were the child; he was the grown-up. He was so much more powerful than you. What do you think would have happened if you refused? Do you really think he would have stopped?" she asked.

"I don't know. Yes, he probably would have stopped." My head was spinning.

"What do you think he was getting out of it? Or, did you think he was just being generous, and doing it for you?"

I never once thought about that perspective before. Actually, I never thought about him getting *anything* from it, period. Certainly, I didn't think about it as a child because I didn't even know that a man's sexual response existed. As I began to question what I knew at that age, Cali's philosophy of remembering things with an adult mind began to come to light.

"Truthfully, I hate to sound like I am defending him or saying anything that excuses what he did. But, I think in his own sick way, he thought he was loving me and making me feel good. I think he believed that he was doing it for me." Agreeing with Cali's expression, even I had to recognize my naiveté as soon as I spoke the words.

"Did he ever have an orgasm when he was touching you?" Hammering me with one new perspective after another, Cali was not letting up for a moment. Despite the discomfort of my ongoing struggles to answer, I was captivated by every door of new thought she was opening.

"No, he didn't." As soon as I uttered the words, I instantly realized that I never would have known if that was happening. At the time, I didn't know about the existence of an orgasm. I had no idea that there was a name for the feeling that I was having, and I was definitely not aware of his physical responses.

"Are you sure? What did he do after you were done? Did he go to the bathroom or did he just remain seated?"

"I can't remember," I replied. I had never thought about what had happened immediately afterwards. Once again, I realized something different. Despite my resistance to Cali's approach, a new and fuller context continued to develop.

"Did he ever get an erection?" Cali asked.

"I don't know. I didn't even know what an erection was at that time, so I wouldn't have noticed. And, even if I did, I'm sure I didn't connect it to anything." Again, Cali pointed out something that had never occurred to me before.

"Do you *really* think he was doing it just for you?" Cali repeated, almost in summation of her tedious, step-by-step approach to dissecting my beliefs.

"Well, maybe not. I don't know. What do you think?" The thoughts and feelings I had held so close for so long were scrambling.

"I think there are a number of possibilities. But, one thing is for sure. He was definitely getting something out of it. Maybe he couldn't get aroused with a grown woman. Maybe he would get up and go masturbate afterwards. There are all sorts of possibilities. But Terry, he wasn't doing it just for you," Cali concluded.

I couldn't believe it. I *could not* believe that Cali was able to tear apart what I had based my self-perception on for years.

"But, what about the fact that I was the one who voluntarily walked over to him?" I asked. In spite of the sense she was making, I was still hanging on to the 25-year opinion with which I was most familiar.

"Well, you don't remember what was said or done before, during, or after he touched you. You can't say whether or not he said, or did, anything that overpowered or coerced you. I would bet anything that he whispered something, looked at you, or intimidated you in some way."

"I was not intimidated."

"Did *you* ever take his hand and put it down your pants?"

"No."

"Was *he* the one who put his hand down your pants?"

"Yes. In fact, I remember how I just wanted a backrub. I used to push his hands away, but eventually, he started to touch me, and then it felt good and I let it happen."

"*You mean YOU* pushed *HIS* hands away?" Cali asked, dismayed by my diminishment of such a pivotal factor.

"Yeah. I still sleep on my stomach in that same guarded position I used to assume, with my arms held tightly against my sides," I replied, sickened by what had become a habitual, nightly reminder.

"And, *he* still kept moving his hand back down your pants?"

"Yes. But, there was a point when I stopped pushing his hands away," I repeated.

"You mean that you became entirely responsible in the few moments after you stopped fighting him? Your blame rests on what? One second? Two? Ten? With no consideration or weight given to *what he did*, your age, the atmosphere, or any of the other contributing factors?"

"Yeah. One second or ten seconds, I shouldn't have succumbed to him," I stubbornly answered, unaware that her question was like the birth of a termite that would eventually eat away the core of my beliefs in the months to come. "The bottom line is that I still knew it was wrong, Cali. He even said to me on a couple of occasions that we had to stop. Sort of like he was telling me that we were going to get in trouble if we didn't. But, things still continued." I could remember exactly where we were standing and how guilt-ridden I felt about myself for being so selfish and weak.

"He set you up, Terry. He made you think it was your fault. Don't you see how he controlled you?"

I was starting to see her point. Perhaps he was more insidious than I permitted myself to remember. Although, if saying it felt like I was excusing myself, then I was not going to admit it.

"I don't know. I just don't know anymore." I was confused. Cali's mission was accomplished. She had taken my long-standing beliefs, thrown them up in the air and blasted them to bits. Months later, I would come to learn that shaking things up into a mass of confusion was the objective for developing different understandings. The first step was to remove my grip from the one-dimensional view I had stubbornly held onto for years. It was the only way to make my feelings more pliable.

As best as I was able, it was the very beginning of understanding the concept of remembering things without an adult mindset. I needed to put myself back into the atmosphere as a ten-year-old, without the choices, knowledge, or life experiences of an adult. After months of work, I was still unconvinced. Yet, I started to entertain the notion that what I knew at 35 was not what I knew when I was 10. This was the first time I ever recalled being presented with logical and valid reasons to support a different perspective about the liabilities of my childhood.

CHAPTER 9

What Haven't You Told Me?

March 2000

"How have you been feeling over the past few weeks?" Cali asked, checking in on my overall well-being.

"Well, I haven't *loved* talking about Louis," I answered, with a humored smirk.

"I know it has been difficult for you. You've done a great job hanging in there. But lately I've been wondering why you always seem so composed. Have you been feeling okay with what we've been talking about?" she asked, instinctually guided in the right direction.

Braving the risk that I would be forced to review the entire series of incidents again if I admitted to my discomfort, I honestly shook my head 'no' in response.

"Really?" Cali looked surprised.

"Yes. I've had unbelievable anxiety for weeks," I admitted.

"Why haven't you shared those feelings with me?"

"Because I've tried to keep things under control. I hate having anxiety attacks, and talking about how they feel only exacerbates the angst," I explained, already feeling the resurgence of palpitations in my chest.

Since we first began to meet, Cali knew there was much left unsaid. However, her hands had previously been tied by the risk that I would walk out of therapy if pushed too far out of my comfort zone.

Clearly, our agreement about hospitalization and my consistent return to her office over the ensuing months demonstrated my intrigue, and a firmer commitment to honesty and the process. Yet, she knew that I still remained unable to venture into arenas in which I felt most uncomfortable. It almost didn't matter what feeling or topic arose. It was crucial to get behind my controlled façade, and it was time for her to chance becoming more assertive.

"So Terry, *what haven't you told me?*" Cali shrewdly asked.

The heat raging through my body felt like it was about to blister my skin. For the very first time in my life, my veneer was destroyed. I didn't realize it then, but in that one moment, my talent for almost complete self-control would *never again* accompany me to Cali's office.

"You're nervous, Terry. What's up?"

"I don't know. My heart is racing and I feel lightheaded," I anxiously replied, as my grip tightened around the arms of the chair.

"Your face is beet red. Would you like some water?" Cali tenderly asked.

"Yes, please," I choked. I didn't know it then, but my complexion would soon become my enduring nemesis.

Cali left the room and returned with a glass of cold water. I needed to steady myself. I noticed my bloodless fingers turning a shade of blue, as my clench strangled away the circulation. One more wave of palpitations and I would be on the floor. Cali sat down across from me and waited until I finished sipping the water.

"Are you okay?" she asked.

"Not really. I'm not sure why this is happening," I replied, startled that I still could not fully regain my composure. I had a thousand thoughts, but my mind could not identify one of them.

"*What haven't you told me?*" Cali unwaveringly repeated. I couldn't recall any other time in my life when my physical response was so irrepressible. She knew she was inside now.

"I don't know. My anxiety is overwhelming, and it feeds off of itself. Whenever I feel lightheaded, I panic that I'm going to have a vertigo attack. It happened a couple of years ago, and it was terrifying. The entire room started spinning, and I couldn't even move," I explained. The short break and the water began to help. Breathing more steadily, I could feel myself beginning to slightly recover.

"How often have you been feeling this anxiety?" Cali asked.

"Too often. It's like I have an anxiety monster living on my shoulder." I thought back to college when I was a die-hard fan of a comic strip that featured a young child who had a big, purple, polka-dotted anxiety monster burst out of his closet every night.

"Why haven't you talked to me about it?" she asked.

"Because, I know if I talk about it, the anxiety will only heighten. Even saying that *I don't* want to talk about it makes it worse. The less I'm aware of it, the better."

"Does not talking about it allow you to become less aware of it?"

"I guess not," I replied, suddenly realizing that of course, I was *always* aware of the things that bothered me. But, prompting a more extensive discussion about my anxiety by admitting this to Dr. Joseph was another matter. "Regardless, it still feels worse to talk about it," I continued.

"It may feel worse at first, Terry. But, I believe in facing your feelings head on, not running from them. Talking about the anxiety over and over again will give you a different understanding of it. If you develop a different understanding, you will eventually feel less anxious," Cali said, attempting to reassure me.

"Yeah, but that doesn't mean I can't hate talking about how I feel," I replied.

"What feelings do you hate talking about?"

"Anxiety and loneliness. Even when I'm with people, I feel alone." I soon learned that the more uncomfortable or anxious I became, the more Cali pushed. What's more, from this session forward, she always knew when to push, as my discomfort was written in red, all over my face.

"Do you ever remember feeling like this before?" she asked.

"Like what?" I stalled.

"Anxious, alone, or anything else you are feeling right

now," Cali sighed, rolling her eyes at having to drag every word out of me.

"Yeah, plenty of times. Except for the years Kurt was healthy, I've probably felt like this most of my life. I've never felt so disconnected," I explained. My face instantly began to flush again. I had always been an expert at creating appearances, choosing when and where to maintain my composure. That was over. My anatomy forced my hand.

"Terry, why are you so anxious? *What haven't you told me?*" she persisted. I could hardly hear her words over the pounding calypso drums that now inhabited the inside of my heart.

"I don't want to say."

"Why not?"

"Because, then it will become true," I replied, surprising myself with the insight. Until I voiced this answer, even I had never been fully aware of this fear.

"I don't understand. Explain that to me," Cali demanded.

"Because saying things out loud is different. If I don't put some of my thoughts into words, I can still hold onto the chance that my beliefs may not be true," I explained. Somehow I had deduced that hearing my thoughts aloud could transform a feeling into a reality.

"But, if you talk about your thoughts, maybe there will be a different way to understand them," Cali suggested.

"There isn't any other way. I already understand exactly what I'm feeling. Believe me Cali, I know certain things about myself, and they are undeniable no matter how you look at them," I insisted.

"There are always other ways. Terry, do you remember how you felt when we first talked about Louis and the abuse? You've felt like this before, but after we talked, your perspectives changed in ways that you hadn't predicted. What are these 'things' that you know about yourself? What are you so afraid to say out loud?"

Anxiety throbbed in every organ of my body. Even my tongue felt like it had a heart of its own. Throughout my adult life, I had numerous experiences with public speaking. Even if I was rattling inside, my complexion had never changed, and I always remained poised. Now, however, I had no choice but to step forward.

"Mostly it's that I am a fraud," I confessed, inhaling deeply.

"What do you mean?"

"I'm not the person that people think I am. There is so much about me that people don't know."

"What don't they know?" Cali asked.

"They don't know how I feel about life or myself. Generally, people think I have my shit together, and that I'm confident and self-assured. I've scammed everyone into believing that I'm someone I'm not," I answered.

"So then tell me, Terry, who are you?" Cali asked.

"I would rather not say."

"Why not?"

"Because, like I told you, once I say it, it will be for real," I repeated.

"You mean that as long as you don't say the words, how you feel won't be real?" Cali would not let up for a moment.

"I suppose," I answered, feeling her reasoning loosen my stronghold.

"Please Terry. I want you to tell me what it is about you that you are so afraid to say," Cali softly pleaded. Her persistent kindness gave me the final push.

"I'm selfish and dishonest," I whispered, slowly peeling back another layer of my appearances.

"Why do you think you are dishonest?" she asked.

"Because I've always needed to feel someone worry about me. When I was younger, I used to pretend or exaggerate things, so that my friends would be concerned. There is definitely something wrong with me." Until the moment the answer rolled off my tongue, I had always planned on taking this "quality" of mine to my grave. I immediately felt my anxiety rise incrementally with every degree of my body temperature.

"Why do you think that makes you dishonest?" Cali was surprisingly unfazed.

"Because, I did those things for attention, and to feel taken care of. My feelings are not truthful if I embellish them."

"Terry, I think if we look closely enough at your history, and the people in your life, you would see that others were not always able to give you what you needed. This isn't a surprise.

Obviously, nobody can get every one of their needs met all the time. But, I think what is remarkable is that you found a way to fill some of them. This does *not* mean you were dishonest. It just means that you found a way to get what you were missing," Cali explained.

"No, Cali. I always felt cared for and loved by the people in my life. I was born with a sickness. I know it," I insisted.

"You could've been cared for and loved, *while at the same time*, had needs that weren't being met. It's not black or white, or either-or, Terry," Cali replied. "What sickness do you think you were born with?"

"I don't know. There's something wrong with me because of the type of person that I am, and the attention that I crave."

"What type of person are you?"

I finally decided to brave my most private, defining character flaw. "It's hard to tell you. But, I guess it doesn't matter because saying it, or not saying it, won't change the fact that it's true," I began, inching out from behind one of my most private walls of self-condemnation.

"What Terry? What's the truth?" Cali softly asked, trying to cushion my turmoil.

"*The truth is that I am a loser.*" My mouth felt like it had produced its own sounds.

"What makes you a loser?" Cali squinted.

"Because, for most of my life, I've been a loner. I was never popular, and I've always been an outsider. I have some characteristics that are innately unattractive or something."

"What characteristics?"

"I'm not sure exactly, but I *know* I was born a certain way. There's something about me that projects the undeniable fact that I'm a loser." Each spoken word created a more foreboding reality. I dreaded having to explain it any further.

"So, what did Kurt see in you? Didn't he really know you?"

"Kurt saw what he wanted to see. I don't know." I was stumped. I had never considered that point of view before. I couldn't even attempt a reasonable explanation.

"Well, it seems important that you figure it out, don't you think?" Cali asked, lunging at the first pivot in my perspective. "Who are your other friends?"

"I have two best friends, Paul and Rose. We've known each other forever, and we're extremely close."

"Well, what do you think *they* see in you?"

"They see the image I've created—that I'm more popular and grounded than I really am."

"Terry, do you think Paul and Rose are fools?"

"What do you mean?" I replied, baffled by the notion.

"Well, they must not be very smart if you've been able to trick them for so long."

"I don't understand."

"In some ways, you're calling them losers, too. Because, how could they like you if *you* are such a loser? How can you have respect for them or their intelligence?" Cali could read the headway she was gaining all over my face. "What do you think *I* see in you?" she relentlessly continued.

"I don't know," I murmured, relieved that she had made the mistake of not insisting that I answer her question about Paul and Rose.

"Do you think that you've tricked me, too?"

"Maybe you're just more tolerant of different personality types because of your profession," I suggested.

"Oh, Terry. Let me tell you something about me that most people who come to this office don't know. I am one of the least tolerant people you'll ever meet. It has *nothing* to do with tolerance. It has *everything* to do with the person I see in front of me. And, it's my job not to be fooled by people's words," Cali clarified. "How can you explain that the people who you respect and admire, can love and care about such a loser?"

I was defenseless. I had no answer. But, I was hooked. Although I was uncomfortable with being backed into a corner, I was exhilarated by the challenge, and the concrete possibilities that there were flaws in my self-perception.

"But the way I feel about myself is based on things that are beyond the opinions of my closest friends, Kurt, or even you. I've had a whole *lifetime* of unwelcome feelings and experiences that support what I'm saying."

Although Cali continued to hit one point after another, the memories of the years I spent feeling rejected, alone or as an outsider were still barricading the doors that had locked in years of unwavering beliefs.

"Were you ever disliked by anyone who mattered to you?" she asked.

"Yeah," I reflexively answered.

"Like who?"

"I don't know. Old boyfriends and people like that. I can't remember anyone specifically right now." Scanning the years without success, I was stunned that I was unable to produce more than a couple of inconsequential names.

"So, let me get this straight, Terry. You are basing the self-perception that you are a loser on the opinions of people that don't even matter to you, rather than on the people who you respect, and who *really* matter?" Cali was kicking down the doors.

"I don't know. Yeah, I guess," I replied. "But, don't you think that, even though those people may not have mattered to me, their opinions are still a partial indicator of how I must appear to others?"

"Only if you are going to give their opinions greater weight than those of your two best friends, your husband, or me," Cali answered, continuing to pry my fingers off the only view of myself that I had ever had.

"I don't know what to think," I replied, more confused than ever. "I know it's hard for you to see, but I *really feel* that I was born with something inside of me that makes me a loser." The battle between my lifelong perceptions and the sensibility of Cali's propositions raged on.

"What do you mean? Do you think you were born with a *loser gene*?" Cali asked incredulously.

"Yeah. That's what I'm saying," I answered. "There is definitely something about me that's inherently unappealing."

"When did you first notice this birth defect?" Cali sarcastically continued.

"I think I first noticed it somewhere around 10 years old, because that was the age when the boys and the girls in my class started to become more friendly." I dreaded going back over the years I spent pretending that I was unaware of, or unaffected by, my alienation from people. "So, it highlighted that I was on the outside of the social circles. I always pretended not to be bothered that I was never one of the popular girls."

"So, you believe that you were born with this loser gene, but it was *dormant* for the first *10 years* of your life?" Cali asked, tirelessly barraging me.

"Yes. No. Well, it was always there, but I wouldn't say it was dormant," I answered, immediately recognizing the absurdity of my theory. "But, maybe there's more to it than a loser gene, anyway," I continued.

"What do you mean?" she asked with eyes of exasperation.

"Because, I'm innately a malcontent. I get bored or uninterested in things so quickly. It's really hard for me to find anything or anyone that I enjoy for any length of time."

"You mean you were born with a *malcontent gene*, too?" Cali's smile spoke to me with that 'you've got to be kidding' expression.

"Yeah," I could barely answer with a straight face. "If I have an interest in something, it's usually fleeting."

"Have you been interested in therapy?"

"Yes."

"How do you explain that?"

"I don't know. This is an exception."

"An *exception to a genetic disorder?*" Cali opened her eyes wide in amazement.

"Yeah," I stubbornly answered, stifling shouts of, 'No, of course not' inside of me. "How else do you explain that I've spent a majority of my life bored and unhappy? I've always felt like dying was better than living. I don't talk about it because I know that no one would understand. But, the feelings are always there—looming over me."

"When was the first time you remember feeling like dying?"

I paused for a few moments, struggling to place a number on the years. "When I was 10," I approximated. "I can't remember exactly when it began, but I distinctly remember being in the fourth grade, walking across the school field, scuffing my heels through the grass, thinking how I couldn't wait until this was over—life, that is."

"Did you ever tell anyone how you were feeling?"

"When?"

"Any time."

"It was a long time ago. It's not a big deal," I protested.

"Well, then, if it isn't a big deal, you should be able to tell me about it."

And on we went again. Cali was locked on. She would never allow me any reprieve from the momentum.

"Even if it's *not* a big deal, that doesn't necessarily make it easier to talk about. Don't you think there are things that happen in your life that are *always* hard to speak of? Besides, even if it *is* a big deal, how I was feeling back when I was 10 years old is irrelevant to how alone I feel today." I didn't want to be in the fourth grade again—even if it was with a one-hour memory in the confines of Dr. Joseph's office.

"Seems 10 years old was a pivotal time for you, huh? Or, is that just an irrelevant coincidence, too?" Cali sarcastically asked.

Suddenly, my exhaustion and dehydration from the night before caught up to me, and the room started to rock from side to side. Dr. Joseph's relentless annihilations and my own surging anxiety attacks had finally strangled away my fortitude.

"What's wrong? Are you feeling okay?" she asked.

"No. I'm just anxious," I replied, straining to prevent myself from passing out. With an increasingly more dreadful recovery, I could no longer hide how sick I was feeling from the spotlight of daytime's public view.

"It's more than that, isn't it?" Cali asked, keeping tempo with the colors of my face.

"I don't know. It's just happening out of nowhere."

"*Come on*, Terry," she urged, circumventing the exercise of extracting my answers again.

"I just don't feel good, and I'm trying not to faint. It's probably from being a little too excessive last night," I replied, immediately regretting opening that door. However, I knew Dr. Joseph could smell an evasion a mile away. Any more avoidance and she would've just locked onto the question with the jaws of a pitbull.

"How were you excessive?" she asked.

"I really didn't plan on it, but I wound up taking a Percocet and having a few too many drinks," I admitted.

"You took a Percocet?" Cali asked. My attempt to downplay it was unsuccessful.

"Yeah. I told you a long time ago that I was taking them on occasion."

"No, Terry, you never mentioned taking them on *any* occasion," Cali insisted.

"Yes, I did. Remember when I came in to see you when Kurt was still alive?"

"Of course, I remember. But, refresh my memory about the Percocets you never mentioned," she sternly requested.

"Come on. I told you about a movie I saw. You know. The one with the nurse who becomes a heroin addict," I began. I had honestly forgotten that I never once mentioned the pills to her before. But, there was no way to un-ring the bell. The information was out there, and there was no turning back.

"Tell me about the movie again."

"It was a movie about a nurse who lived and worked in a ghetto. She treated victims of shootings and drug overdoses every day. There was no way for her to escape the daily horrors, because she had no money and couldn't take time off. Her boyfriend found track marks on her arms, and wanted to help her get clean. But, she refused. She didn't want to stop because being high was the only trip she could take away from it all. That's how I've felt. So much of my life was inescapable when Kurt was sick. I needed a break, and Percocets were my vacation." I knew Kurt was deteriorating, but my personal well-being had taken a ride right down with each dying nerve.

"Terry, the difference is that Kurt is *not* here anymore, and there are so many other ways to take a break *without* drugs," Cali responded. "What have you been doing?"

"I don't know. It's always different. I usually have a few drinks to relax. It's not like I ever plan on it. Some nights I just take one, and others I might take a couple."

"Let me get this straight. When I've suggested anti-depressant medication, you've continually refused it because you say that you don't want to feel artificial. But, you self-medicate yourself with a potentially lethal combination of alcohol and narcotics?"

"It's different, Cali. I'm not taking them every day. In fact, I *never* take them during the day. It's only at night, and almost always when I'm home alone. It's not a big deal. It's under control." As the words left my mouth, I began to have my very first uneasy feelings about my private world of substances and the rationalizations that my short-term sabbaticals from reality were without consequences.

I was well aware of the fact that I had continually concealed my hangovers whenever I entered Cali's office. But it suddenly became notable that I had never spoken to her, or *anyone* else, about the presence of Percocets in my life—a perilous omission for which the reasons were more evident than I was willing to admit.

What began as one simple question, "What haven't you told me?" had developed into a succession of enlightening inquiries, including that I had long since deleted the prefix from painkiller. Not talking about it had permitted me to perpetuate guilt-free indulgences without having to concede that I had long since crossed the boundary line demarcating abuse. Apparently even I was unaware of what I was *not* saying—including what I was *not* telling myself.

CHAPTER 10

The Key

May 2000

Working together in Dr. Joseph's office began to resemble the dance that followed stepping up together onto the platform of a trapeze. There had been enough suicidal references for her to recognize I was in danger. It had become imperative to flush out as many details as possible about both my drug use and the extent to which I desired to die. But, she also realized that in order to uncover the threat that was being posed, there had to be some sense of surety that I wasn't going to overdose if pushed too far. I was walking on a tight rope without a netted catch below. A miniscule slip one way or the other and I was finished.

"What's up?" Cali began as I took a seat across from her.

"Nothing. I'm not feeling very good today. I really shouldn't have those things around," I answered.

"What things? The Percocets?" Cali asked.

"Yeah. I just needed to kill the anxiety."

"Did they help you feel less anxious?"

"Yes, definitely," I said.

"Do you think there were any costs to that?" she asked.

"I don't know. I guess having to deal with feeling this sick for the next few days is a price to pay," I answered.

"What other costs are there?" Cali continued.

"Well, I'm upset because I told myself that I wouldn't be excessive again." A vision of the empty bottle of wine, I hardly recalled finishing off, flashed before my eyes.

"Are there any other costs?" Cali persisted.

"No," I answered, annoyed at being repeatedly asked the same question.

Cali rarely stopped with my first response. It took me a long time before I understood the purpose. I had certainly given enough of an answer to move onto a different question. But Cali was digging deep into the cavernous exploration of my mind, and no psychological stone was going to be left unturned. Each time the question was repeated, I was forced to reach further inside of myself, and disclose things I otherwise would have either abridged or avoided in entirety. Although it would have been much easier had Dr. Joseph guided me along with a lecture about the list of costs, it would have circumvented a significant part of the process. There was also much more to be gained by forcing me to stretch my mind until *I* could produce, and more importantly, *feel*, my own words.

"Think about it, Terry. Do you think there is a cost to you and me?"

"No," I replied, fighting the wedge she was hammering in between the drugs and me.

"How many Percocets did you take last night?"

"I would rather not talk about it." Other than washing them down with a gulp of wine, I could barely remember.

"Do you think that *not* telling me is a cost?"

"Yeah, I suppose," I murmured.

"How is it a cost?" Cali tediously continued.

"I suppose it limits what we discuss. But mostly I think it affects us because of how sick I feel. Lightheadedness makes me even more anxious, and I'm less able to concentrate."

"So, would you agree that it *does* interfere with the process?"

"Yes," I had to admit. "But the anxiety I live with is too much to take. When I get high, everything I'm feeling gets diffused. I don't have to think. That's all I want—to just *stop* my mind and not have to think," I explained. For more occasions than I cared to remember, I had been short-circuiting the sixth gear of my brain, which had been racing along in overdrive ever since I was old enough to know I was alive.

"What don't you want to think about?" Cali asked.

"I don't know. Lots of stuff," I replied.

"That doesn't tell me much, Terry. You don't have to list every single thing. Just start somewhere—anywhere," Cali suggested.

"It's just a swirl of things. Everything comes at me all at once," I answered.

"Well, try to be more specific. Just pick one thing.

Anything. What do you think about most often?"

I paused for a few silent moments. A pin dropping several miles away could've been heard.

"Dying," I said under my breath. Even the *thought* of speaking my reply accelerated the blood flow through my body, opening every vein into its own miniature fire hose.

"Have you thought about dying recently?"

"Yeah," I replied, eyes to the floor.

"When?"

"I don't want to say," I answered, another rush of anxiety was painted across my face.

"Why are you so anxious?" she asked.

"I would really rather not say, Cali. It's a huge risk for me to be totally honest." Everything inside me was screaming for the safety of silence. I was torn. I knew I needed to talk to Cali about what I was feeling. However, exposing the extent of my despair was like taking a leap across the most terrifying chasm between trust and self-destruction.

"What's the risk? What could happen?"

"That something involuntary will happen to me," I replied reticently.

"Do we need to review our agreement about hospitalization again? Do you remember what we promised each other?" Of course I remembered. Trusting it was another matter.

"I remember. But, it's still really hard for me to talk about how I'm feeling."

"I understand that it must be very scary for you. But, we have to be able to trust each other." The reddish tint of my face turned to a dark burgundy. "What's happening, Terry? Why are you so anxious?"

"I can feel another blow out coming on this weekend," I confessed.

"Why? What's happening this weekend?"

"Saturday would've been my fourth wedding anniversary. I just want to be able to relax my mind, but I know where that leads," I explained, with visions of another kitchen-center-island obliteration.

"What do you think happens to everything you're feeling when you drink or take Percocets to 'relax' your mind?" Cali asked.

"I feel calmer," I responded.

"Do you think there are any costs to that?"

"No. It really helps me to stop thinking," I stubbornly replied, continuing to oppose Dr. Joseph's tenacious "cost theme" of the session.

"Do you stop thinking about what's bothering you when you get high?"

"Yes, that's the point. I *don't* want to think about *anything.*" Alienating myself from myself was the objective.

"Do you think you sacrifice anything when you stop your thinking process?" Cali persisted.

"Not if I can stop thinking terrible things."

"Terry, don't you see how much we miss when you numb all your thoughts away? How can we figure out what you're feeling if you cut off the process? There is so much to learn if you stay with it, and just work it for a while." Once again, Cali's flow of questioning revealed another irrefutable consequence.

"Yeah, but I don't know if that is such a good idea, Cali. Whenever I get that upset, I just want to die. At least it helps me to get through those times. This is going to be a tough weekend. I can just feel it," I explained.

"Is there anything I can do to help you through the weekend?" she asked, with a disarming softness that made it almost impossible for me to be obstinately resistant. Oddly, I sometimes wished that Cali would just tell me what to do. But, somehow giving me the feeling that I was participating in the choices rather than pushing me back against a wall with a set of demands, made me more inclined to talk about it and more inclined to try to work something out.

"I don't think there's much that can be done to help me. It's not necessarily even about my anniversary, or this weekend. It seems that I'm always fighting to drown the overall feeling of just wanting to die," I despondently replied.

"Terry, there are always ways to help you. You don't have to 'drown' anything you're feeling. We just need to continue talking until we figure something out. There are *always* other options," she emphatically explained. "Is there anything you can think of that would be helpful to you this weekend?"

"I guess one thing is to make sure I don't overdo it again," I proposed.

"Will you throw the pills away?" Cali asked.

"No."

"Will you give them to me?"

"No."

"Isn't there anything we can do?"

"I don't know," I answered, embroiled in a struggle between wanting to walk out of there without any weekend restraints, and wishing she would *do* something, *say* something, *anything*, that would prevent me from feeling so desperately alone and unguarded. Expecting her exasperation, I saw Cali's soft expression. The continued compassion in her voice was a comforting surprise.

"Where are the drugs now?"

"They are locked in a file cabinet at my house," I hesitantly disclosed.

"How about if you give me the key?" Cali suggested.

"No, I don't want to do that. It wouldn't be enough to help me, anyway." I had no intention of relinquishing control of my supply, or giving her the opportunity to destroy the means by which, for years, I had planned my final escape.

"What would be enough to help you?" she asked.

"Probably, if I made you a promise not to get high," I said.

"I see," Cali paused for a moment. "Would you be able to keep that promise?"

"Yes, definitely," I answered.

"How are you so sure?"

"Because, I'm not going to lie to you. If I promise you something, then I will keep my word."

"Why is keeping your word so important to you?" Cali asked.

"Trustworthiness is critical to me. It's the measurement of who I am," I began. "I grew up with people who rarely honored their word. Confidences were not respected, and I could never depend on a promise not to repeat even the most personal things. So, I have no tolerance for it. It doesn't matter how important, or inconsequential, the commitment might seem. I couldn't sleep at night if I didn't keep my promises. It would haunt me all the time. Besides, being honest with you is especially important to me," I replied.

"Why?" Cali asked.

"Because I'm in therapy to help myself, not to play games about winning or losing. The way I look at it, being deceitful with you does not mean I'm getting away with anything. It makes no sense to put you in a position where you have to police me, and then start lying or hiding things from you. I promised myself that I would be totally honest with you about everything we discuss—no matter how difficult it is. If I can't be honest, I would rather not say anything at all," I explained. "But, I just don't want to give you the drugs."

"It doesn't have to be all or nothing, Terry. Can't we reach a compromise?"

"I don't think there is one," I replied, in my uniform of pessimism.

"I want to do whatever is necessary to make sure you are safe, Terry. So, let's talk about a promise, okay?"

"Sure."

"Can you give me the key, with a promise that you won't take anything, *just* for this weekend? And, I will promise to return the key when we meet again next week," Cali proposed.

"I don't know. I'm afraid to agree to anything unless I can truthfully say that I can keep my promise," I replied.

"You've never been dishonest with me, Terry. I trust you. And, you can trust me. I promise that I will never lie to you. Why don't we just give it a try for this weekend?" she asked.

"Okay," I finally agreed. Despite my fears, it seemed like a reasonable and tolerable start.

It wasn't until much later in the process that I realized I had conceded to a cleverly constructed, back door demand. Cali made it look like the weekend promise and handing over the key was my decision. While she maintained the appearance of merely proposing the agreement, she had already made up her mind that, one way or another, I was, at the very least, going to hand over the key. She created a dialogue in which I felt like a participant rather than a subordinate, and her aura of sincerity fostered my cooperation.

"When will you bring me the key?" Cali pulled the reigns in too tight for me to wriggle away with any loose-ended agreements.

"I'll drop it off tomorrow," I replied.

"Do you know what's at stake here?" Cali relentlessly continued.

"Yes," I answered, not wanting to review the list that I knew would unavoidably seal the deal.

"Tell me what's at stake," she persisted.

"Your license," I said. It pained me to reply. Every stated reason secured our agreement with the stamp of my conscience, and created that much more of a distance from the reprieve of the drugs.

"Yes, that's true, and it's not insignificant to me. But, more importantly, what is at stake for you?" she asked, clearly with something more specific in mind.

"Our relationship," I guessed.

"No, Terry. If you ever broke your promise, we would have to deal with the issue of trusting one another, again. But, there is absolutely *nothing* you could do that would destroy our relationship, or make me kick you out of therapy. And, I'll tolerate the risk to my license, and whatever else I have to do in order to help you. *What is at stake, Terry?*" she implored.

"I don't know."

"*Your life, Terry*. Your *life* is what's at stakc."

I was speechless. I was well aware that most therapists would never have been able to tolerate the risks, or even consider entering this type of agreement with the key. It would have been perfectly understandable to me, had she been principally concerned with protecting her own interests. But, I finally realized she was not like the others. Her concern was not about protecting her career. Rather, her primary focus was to save my life. And, it was because of this awareness that I was able to cross the threshold of trusting the sincerity of her commitment. I was worth enough for her to take the risks.

Opening up the vault of my brain was no easy task. It was rather interesting that a small, metal key became the representation of so many parts of myself. Handing it to Cali was not only a commitment to remain clean, but it was a bold statement that it was time to lock up the drugs and unlock my mind. A Percocet had become worth a million words.

CHAPTER 11

It is the Getting There

June 2000

The spring of 2000 was in full bloom. My anxiety was like a weed, popping up more often than the tulips. Although essential to our ability to move forward, handing over the key, and making a promise to get through my first anniversary weekend without Kurt fell far short of a panacea. In fact, it was only the beginning of months of arduous struggles that became the focus of the bulk of our sessions.

Although I repeatedly refused a full surrender of my stash, Cali never gave up the fight. She continued to keep her promises to return the key. Somehow, she managed to tolerate the risks of my refusals to hand it back over, while tenaciously pursuing a series of compromises for more short-term resolutions—always with the goal of someday securing a permanent solution to help me. For the time being, her work resembled emptying the water out of a sinking boat, so that it would have the capacity to take on more water until it was repaired.

Cali had to work around her inability to present me with the ultimatum that I either agree to complete sobriety or terminate treatment. She instead proceeded more carefully, realizing that our progress would have to come in the form of smaller steps—steps that hinged on having me remain present in her office rather than risk that I would discontinue therapy. Some opportunity to reach me was better than no opportunity. Cali sustained a tempo that kept the delicate balance between remaining prudently patient, and becoming effectively aggressive. She cautiously pursued agreements for one day, one weekend, or any segment of time that she could persuade me to hand over the key and ensure my safety with a promise to remain straight.

Trust in the sanctimony of our promises became a critical prerequisite to our work together under these conditions. Each time Cali held the key, she immediately returned it to me upon my request—as she had promised. I, on the other hand, could barely contain my desire to numb myself into unconsciousness. I filled the time between re-exchanging the key with one blow out after another, leading us into what became a series of routine negotiations. Drug treatment was suggested, but I refuted any notion that I was addicted—even to the extent of objecting to the use of the term "addiction" during our appointments. *Recreational over-consumption* was palatable, but *drug addiction* was entirely unacceptable.

Cali soon underscored stubbornness as one of my most ingrained personality traits, as I remained particularly sensitive to her phraseology. A list of alternative and restricted vocabulary began to develop. I was *excessive*, not *addicted*. I *wanted* to get high, I did not *need* to get high. I had a *problematic childhood*, but I was not *abused*. My excessive worrying was not *obsessing*, I was *anxious* with an *over-active* mind. I was not *clinically depressed*, I was *innately apathetic*. I was not in need of anti-depressant medication, I was an *untreatable, genetically-based malcontent*.

As our work continued through the spring, and well into the summer months, Cali and I could only dance around the underlying reasons for which I was annihilating myself. It took many months for me to accept that my distress was in fact a culmination of the tentacles of all the prior experiences of my life. Instead, it seemed we were constantly absorbed by the distraction of resolving the drug issues, bargaining over promises, and keeping me safe. At first glance, it appeared that much time was being wasted on extraneous issues, rather than focusing on the more standard, therapeutic discussions about my current feelings, and the specific events of my life. However, Cali taught me an invaluable lesson about the usefulness of each and every one of our communications. It was an insight that became essential to maintaining my commitment to continue therapy during that period of time.

It began with an analogy Cali made, using a movie we both had seen about a boy who had attempted suicide. The boy had been meeting with his psychologist for months without any apparent progress. One night, the boy became hysterical and called his therapist. They met at the therapist's office, in the middle of the night, for what Dr. Joseph referred to as the "Ah Ha!" session. As the boy sat there crying and confused about the root of his hysteria, the therapist dropped his typically soft-handed approach and aggressively pressed him to face why he was filled with such self-hatred. The boy broke down into the arms of his therapist as he suddenly realized he was not to blame for his friend's death—the event that precipitated his earlier suicide attempt. The scene was portrayed as his one-hour, cure-all "Ah Ha!" session. That is, a sudden realization that brought all the pieces of his problems together. While understandably abbreviated and happily ended for the purposes of Hollywood, Cali explained why it was not applicable to the realities of our journey.

"It is the *getting* there that is just as important as the *arriving* there," Cali stated. It was a simply stated philosophy, but it spoke volumes to me about the meaningfulness of our elongated battles that had the appearance of being superfluous to the "real" work. Essentially, our immersion in the process of *getting* to the more customary, therapeutic destinations WAS the work.

117

It was a pivotal lesson that couldn't have come at a better time. I had begun to feel the frustration of spending months in what seemed like ineffectual discussions about promises and drugs. I was continuing to teeter in and out of my commitment to remain in therapy. Refusing to promise abstinence, promising not to be excessive and then consequently becoming excessive again, repeatedly having a discussion about that excessiveness and then reaffirming new promises to remain straight and safe had become a dizzying, repetitive, and time-consuming cycle. In the meantime, I continued to live in the depths of despair, and I was growing less and less hopeful that there was anything that would ever alleviate my anguish. Consequently, it was through the creation of this very understanding about the mechanics of the process that Cali helped me to hold onto some faith that our work together was nevertheless progressive and worthwhile.

Contrary to the movies, even if it did not appear as though we had experienced the immediate remedy of the all-awakening, Hollywood version of the "Ah Ha!" session, we were building upon our relationship and the establishment of mutual trust—an indispensable requirement for the times we were to face ahead. We were ironing out agreements, and I was learning how to compromise, or persevere, until we figured out ways in which to work out even the most seemingly irresolvable issues.

Moreover, we were gathering piecemeal understandings that would inevitably contribute to helping me reach my goal of remaining comfortably alive. Perhaps there would come a day, or many days, where we would arrive at conclusive, "Ah-ha!" understandings, but in the interim, it was going to be a work in progress. Every single one of our conversations was an integral prelude to the next—each one of them an inseparable and invaluable part of the continuum that comprised the therapeutic process.

Once again, Dr. Joseph's caring mannerisms and her ability to articulate a new perspective succeeded in encouraging me to return to her office for ongoing treatment. As Cali tightened the buckle around my seat, for the first time I began to appreciate the multi-dimensional benefits of the work we were achieving through the vehicle of *getting there*.

CHAPTER 12

The Everything Bagel

July 2000

The simple choice of where to sit while I took the first bite into my freshly baked, morning bagel triggered the beginning of one of the most powerful transformational momentums to occur during the course of my treatment with Dr. Joseph.

I arrived at WP's, a local bagel shop, during the mid-morning rush. I chose a seat in front of the oversized, plate glass windows that looked out onto the parking lot in front of the store. Newspaper, coffee, and my "everything bagel" in hand, I chose a seat in the hot, summer, morning sun that was streaming through the front windows. I began to review the headlines to pass some of the time.

The days of the week had blended into one, distinguished only by the time in between my appointments with Dr. Joseph. Plans or no plans, I existed alone in a place in which the presence of an army of people could not have provided me with any company. The warmth of summer's revival no longer brought me its traditional reprieve. Enthusiasm had become a stranger. Food no longer had any appetizing flavors. I was just going through the motions.

I busied myself with anything I could find in order to avoid looking at the handsome, young couple standing in line, with their fingers affectionately interlocked—a heavily weighted reminder of my solitude and the happiness with Kurt that I had watched slip from my grasp.

I had left Dr. Joseph's office the previous day, with the key in my pocket, and another refusal to make a promise to remain drug-free for the weekend. As I sat there, staring blankly at the print on the newspaper, I was entirely consumed with the debate over whether or not I would ever be able to make her that promise again, or just resume the cycle of my usual, life-threatening self-indulgences. Ironically, it was because of that very preoccupation that I stopped to take the first bite into *my everything bagel*. As I raised it to my mouth, I lifted up my head and glanced out into the parking lot. Precisely at that moment, a car pulled over, directly in front of me, to drop off a young girl so that she could run inside and buy some bagels.

Suddenly, my breathing came to an abrupt halt, as my heart furiously pumped all the blood in my body away from my head. With only an inch of plate glass and a few feet to separate us, there sat Dr. Joseph in the driver's seat of a convertible.

I had never seen Dr. Joseph out of her office attire before, and knew very little about her personal life. As the skinny little girl jumped out of the passenger side, my reflexes took over, and I instantly leaped back away from the window. I was almost certain that Cali had seen me, but it didn't matter. I couldn't think, I didn't think. I just reacted. I dashed over to the far corner of the crowded store, and stood behind the obstruction of the condiment table. I couldn't even bring myself to look back out the window towards Cali's car. Peering through the small crack of the shelving that separated us, I did not re-emerge until the girl returned to the car, and I could see them drive away.

My heart sank into the pit of my stomach. I was in shock. I was consumed with an overwhelming sense of jealousy and inexplicable envy. Adding to my terrible confusion was the most illogical, emotional paradox. Although I had just fled in the other direction, there was no place in the world

I would've rather been than sitting in that passenger seat. I hadn't the slightest idea what was happening to me. Suddenly, the deliberation over my cyclical weekend promises was secondary to a new wave of emotions. A few months later, I learned it was an event that would change the entire course of my therapeutic journey.

On Monday morning, I embarrassingly returned for my next appointment. I had spent the remainder of the weekend wondering how I was going to explain myself. Given the proximity, I assumed that there was no doubt Dr. Joseph had spotted me. I agonized over whether or not I would be able save face and lie that I didn't see her. I waited for the moment to come, but to my relief, Cali never said a word to me. I was so frightened and disturbed by my reaction that I didn't dare mention anything about it.

As our work continued, the yet-to-be-understood significance of the WP's *everything bagel* day began to spread its tentacles around me. Of course, *not* talking about it insured my confusion, but I was too trapped by my fears to move. Despite my unrelenting sense of isolation, I felt the uninvited emergence of emotional attachment.

Historically, the only true relief I experienced appeared in the form of swallowing small, round, tranquilizing objects. Suddenly, I started to become acutely aware of the emotional shelter provided by Dr. Joseph's care. Unknowingly, a substitute for my usual outlet for comfort had begun. It wasn't until that very moment, on the chair at WP's, that I even began to contemplate how all of our talking during the preceding months of appointments had cultivated a deeply felt attachment—a gnawing array of feelings that began to pervade all our future sessions. Even though I didn't yet understand what was happening, a subtle yet profound transformation had begun to take place. In spite of myself, I became less resistant to returning to Dr. Joseph's office. I didn't know it then, but compliments of WP's bagel shop, I was digesting a bite into my *"starting to feel everything"* bagel.

CHAPTER 13

A Whole Heart

August 2000

As time wore on, I became less and less able to enter into any enduring agreements. All of my actions were increasingly unstable. I gave Dr. Joseph the key, and then I took it back. I stayed straight, and then I blacked out. I continued to schedule appointments, and then I announced I was terminating therapy. My behavior was so erratic that I had become a foreigner to myself.

Each time I worked up the courage to cancel an appointment, I agonized about leaving, and hoped Cali would insist upon my return. I found comfort in her company. Yet, I continued to resist any psychological dependence on her, and struggled to conceal my growing attachment.

Although I counted the days until I could return to the safe haven of her office, I began to dread the repetitive discussions about my safety that would ensue during each and every appointment. Cali urged me to consult an addiction counselor, but I refused. She relentlessly asked for my promise to remain straight, or for a return of the key. It was an exhausting debate that I could not win with any fair degree of logic. Inevitably, I wound up handing the key back over with short-term agreements.

I continuously fought the temptation to break my word. Whenever it bordered on unbearable, I would have Cali paged. We would talk through what I was feeling until I was reminded of the costs to bear if I proceeded to drink or get high.

Unfortunately, it wasn't much further into the summer when my unyielding deliberation over whether to live or die began to devour me. One Sunday afternoon, I reached the limits of my fortitude, and called a locksmith. After several hours of staring into the opened file cabinet of drugs, my conscience and the honor of my word prevailed. I closed the cabinet and immediately had Dr. Joseph paged.

It was the end of the weekend. I expected nothing more than some time with her on the telephone. However, Cali recognized the impending urgency, and within one hour, I was sitting across from her, confessing to what I had done.

We spoke at length about what triggered that particular day's nose-dive. I had been alone during a gorgeous summer day, and I could hardly endure the torment of my loneliness, and the suffocating anguish of missing Kurt. We disputed my belief that I was genetically predestined to a life of misery, and we proceeded to what had almost become our scripted debate about the costs of my actions. Except this time, there was a significant alteration to the dialogue.

As I was in the midst of explaining why death seemed so relieving to me, Dr. Joseph interrupted—a rarity given how increasingly difficult it had become for me to even *begin* speaking about my pain.

"Do you know how much I care about you? *I would have a hole in my heart forever if you died*," Cali declared, staring directly into me with a distinctive softness in her eyes.

"Yeah," I quietly responded, as I struggled to catch my breath. I hadn't the slightest idea why I was feeling so emotional. All I knew was that the wind had been knocked out of me with the conveyance of one, simply-worded, personalized feeling.

I was stunned that she cared about me, and even more astonished that she would actually say so. I had always assumed that the expression of personalized feelings were somehow harmful to the process, and forbidden by the professional parameters of psychotherapy. To the contrary, I found that Dr. Joseph's feelings were the most helpful words I could've heard that day. However, for reasons that did not become known to me for some time, I concealed my reaction, and continued on with our discussion.

Although comforted by the safety of Cali's genuine concern, regrettably, even after another round of tiresome debates, I stubbornly refused to make another promise. I wanted to retain the ability to numb myself into oblivion without restraint, even though the need for Cali to take care of me was on the rise. Her availability and compassion had been enough to pull me away from death's door on that particular day. Thus, feeling somewhat better, I felt confident that I could return home with the key, and moderate my consumption.

A few days later, I wandered back into Dr. Joseph's office in another post-blow out stupor.

"How long do you think it will take you to recover *this time*?" she asked.

"Probably a couple of days."

"Terry, the drugs are ruling your life."

"They are *not*," I sharply rebutted.

"How often do you think you are getting high?"

"I don't know. Probably a couple of times a week," I replied.

"So, between the couple of times per week you are getting high, and the couple of days you feel sick afterwards, you're either high, or you're recovering from being high, a majority of the time?" Cali pointed out.

"No," I answered, trying to do the math.

"Terry, *first* we need to know *what* you are feeling, and we can't know *what* you are feeling if you continue to get high and run. Besides, you can't run forever," Cali stated.

There was no need for a reply. The dangers of excessiveness were written all over the paleness of my face. Several moments passed.

"What are you thinking?" Cali asked, pulling me out from behind a wall of silence.

"I'm afraid that if I don't have the drugs, I'll lose my option to die."

"I understand that you need to *know* it's a door you can open. It's *acting* on it that's another matter," Cali explained with perhaps one of her most powerful, non-threatening statements to date. "I want the chance to talk to you about dying, so that you can see you are *not* alone, and that it's an option you should *never* exercise. I want to help you, Terry. *But I won't become part of your plan to die.*"

My emotional detachment had been riddled with lethal permissibility. But, despite my inclination to run in the other direction, I was thankful for her efforts to erode my rationalization that I could live or die in a vacuum. I realized how Dr. Joseph's startling disclosure about the hole I would've left in her heart had strengthened my connection to her and the work. I needed her to care and to encourage me to remain in therapy until I could embrace the hope she had for my future.

I was relieved by the expression of her personalized feelings, as though they somehow rescued me from myself. Any fear, any statement, any feeling that kept me alive was a successful contribution to the process.

CHAPTER 14

Cyberspace

September 2000

Although I had increased my sessions with Dr. Joseph to twice a week, the days between them had begun to move in agonizing, slow motion. I longed to return to Dr. Joseph's office, while at the same time, I wished more than anything that I would never lay eyes on her again. Even at my best, I could not make any sense of the contradiction. Consistent with every other self-destructive choice I seemed to be making at the time, I decided the best course was to avoid how I was feeling and leave therapy.

"I can't come in anymore," I declared.

"Why not?" Dr. Joseph asked, bewildered.

"Because, it's just not working for me."

"You mean this process isn't helpful to you?"

"No, it's not that. It's just not going to work," I repeated, attempting to remain honest, yet evasive about my weekly desperation to make it to my next appointment.

"Do you want to make this decision alone, or do you want to have someone alongside of you?" Cali asked.

"You can't be alongside of me for this, Cali," I replied, wondering how she could continue to come up with the precise, compassionate words needed to reach me. At that moment, I wanted nothing more than the shelter of her company.

"What are you not telling me?" This question had become an emotional switch that instantly flicked on a rush of uncontrollable anxiety. I sat in silence, unsuccessfully attempting to conceal my reaction.

"There is something there," Dr. Joseph pointed out, directed by the color of my face. "What are you running from, Terry?" She was never going to accept my decision to terminate therapy without discussion.

"Nothing. I just don't want it to matter."

"*What* don't you want to matter? What is it?" she asked.

"I don't know. I can't say," I replied, overcome with confusion. If I wanted to be there, why was I desperately trying to find a way to be rid of her? All I knew was that my instincts were screaming to immediately shut down an overwhelming, inexplicable need to be in her office.

"Is there anything that I'm doing wrong? Please tell me, Terry. I want you to talk to me." Cali's kindness was making it increasingly impossible for me to stand firm with my decision.

"You aren't doing anything wrong. It's me, and it doesn't matter if we talk about it because it's not something that can be changed." I hated the emerging feeling that her pursuit was the very thing I wanted most. Cali's disarming responses kept tipping the scales. The discomfort of staying in therapy, and dealing with those feelings, began to outweigh the dread of leaving.

"What can I do to make it easier for you to tell me? What is it that you need from me, Terry?" Cali gently prodded.

Need. There it was. One simple word began to clarify so much. Despite my desire to make an uncontested, one-dimensional decision, her questions had hooked me, and my conflict began to reconcile.

Sitting inside the four walls of Dr. Joseph's office had become the only place I didn't feel alone. It had become the only safety zone where I could withstand the magnetic pull of death. But the reason I wanted to run was not her office. Nor was it the process, or the therapy itself. It was the resurgence of the *everything bagel* day. It was Cali. I *needed* Cali. Unknowingly, having her care about me had become critical, but I was terrified of the dependency and the exposure intrinsic to personal attachment. I struggled to brave the risk of confessing my feelings, but my tongue was held hostage by my fears. I simply could not speak.

"Do you think you could write your thoughts to me?" Cali suggested.

"Yeah, probably," I replied, struck by the alternative. She couldn't have thought of a better solution. Writing had always come easier for me. I never considered that it would be a permissible supplement to our sessions. Conventional or not, Cali was willing to utilize any means of communication possible in order to secure my return.

As I stood up to leave, Cali scribbled down her e-mail address. Still unaware of its impending influence, by the time I reached my car I could feel the slip of paper burning a hole in my pocket. Neither of us realized it at the time, but this very simple suggestion propelled one of the most powerful momentums to occur during our journey together.

Hitting the send button became one of the most difficult choices I ever made. It was 5:30 in the morning, and I had just completed transcribing needs that even I had been too embarrassed to admit to myself. At the outset, I had no idea what was going to come out of my fingertips. Many months later, I discovered that the pull of the keyboard had thrown me a lifeline. I spent the day waiting for Cali's response. There was no turning back. My fears had already traveled through the irreversible route of cyberspace.

5:13 A.M.

Dear Cali,

I've been sitting in front of my computer for hours, attempting an opening sentence. I think the best way to start is to tell you about a few things that have recently happened.

Not long ago, you made a statement that had a very profound impact on me. I was bottoming out and we were talking about how terrible I was feeling at the time. In the middle of saying something, you interrupted me and stated, "Do you have any idea how much I care about you?" Although I didn't show it, I was stunned. In fact, I spent the next few minutes fighting back tears, just trying to stay focused. It was not so much the statement itself. It was how you said it, your timing, and your expression. You very rarely interrupt me, and obviously you felt a strong enough urge to make your feelings known. I know it may seem rather insignificant, but whenever I've wavered on continuing therapy, that statement is probably what has kept me coming in ever since. I wanted to tell you how much it affected me, but I couldn't because I felt too vulnerable.

*Then during the summer, I saw you at WP's bagels. I was
sitting by the plate glass window that looks out onto the
parking lot, eating a bagel. You pulled up directly in front of
me. It literally took my breath away. I had to get up and walk
to the other side of the store until you drove off. It took me a
few days to recover from that—no kidding. I was sure you saw
me, and wondered how I was going to explain my reaction
(since I couldn't even explain it to myself). But, apparently
you didn't see me, because you never brought it up. At that
moment, I began to realize how much I actually missed you
when I didn't see you.*

*Recently, I changed my mind about terminating therapy. Later
on, when we talked about my decision to remain in treatment,
I claimed that I didn't remember what you said that persuaded
me to stay. But I did remember. I suppose I was just too
embarrassed to admit to the details that made such a difference
to me. You told me again how much you cared about me. You
reminded me that we could work out whatever it was that was
making it so difficult for me to come in. But, most important to
me at the time, you stated that you weren't going to let me go.*

*Given these experiences, here is my theory about what I've
been feeling:*

*I know our relationship is mostly business for you, and I fully
understand the therapeutic boundaries. When you asked me
why I thought the issue concerning my neediness could not
be worked out, I couldn't answer you at the time. But now I
know. It's because you are not my mentor, or my friend (in the
normal sense). Rather, our relationship is strictly professional
on most levels. Thus, I'm always reminding myself that I
need to break away from the attachment I feel toward you,
because I am always going to remain on the outside of your
life. Compounding the problem is the disappointment I feel
in myself for allowing any of these emotions to even begin to*

build. Especially (and with all due respect) with a therapist—a place where it is clear that there are limitations.

I'm stuck in this very painful wish for something that can never be and therefore, I don't want it to be at all. I cannot allow myself to need you. I don't want to have these feelings, nor do I want how much YOU care about me to matter. Inevitably, I will feel so much pain that it will outweigh just about any other benefit at this time.

I've never felt as vulnerable, and yes, scared, as I do right now—not just by writing this, but by allowing myself to even think about it in words. I know that talking about this will make it true. <u>That is, it will confirm to me that the limitations are true, and it is a truth that leaves me even more alone.</u> That is probably the most important sentence of these pages. It's the kind of alone that is far worse than other types, because I'm continually reminded of what I'm missing and what I cannot have in my life. I must keep what I want and need in check, and always remain prepared for our inevitable goodbye.

Even though it terrifies me to be this wide open, I want to be honest with you about what has really been on my mind. So, I'm going to resist the temptation to edit this, and send it off just as I felt it.

Terry

3:14 P.M.

Terry,

It is indeed a gift to hear from your honest "unedited" self, and I first want to tell you how much it means to me. It isn't the words you have sent, although those certainly are profoundly significant, but the feelings behind the words that are so incredibly important.

It is your dilemma that I want very much to help you with, and where you feel stuck, I feel limitless possibility. This incredible self-reflective journey that you are on, and that I have had the privilege to be a part of, has very little to do with business. It has more to do with believing in you, even when you don't believe in yourself. I never lose sight of your capacities. I will fight with everything I have to make sure that you feel them, too, and hope that they will help sustain you during rough times. When you don't believe in yourself, I will fight to remind you of when you did, or when you might, or whatever it would take to make you hold on.

As you reminded me of something I had previously said, I have absolutely no intention of letting you go—until you are ready to leave. And, if you were nearby, I would lean forward, look you in the eye, and tell you that I WILL NOT LET YOU GO. This has more to do with your incredible capacity to not only survive but to live, to LIVE, Terry, than it has anything to do with me.

You are right. I cannot be your mentor, or even your friend, in the traditional sense of the word. All of those relationships have both pragmatic as well as emotional limitations inherent to them, as does any relationship. However, you fail to see that our very unique relationship, while clearly having boundaries, also has an almost limitless potential for connectedness.

You write a critical line, "It will confirm to me that the limitations are true and it is a truth that leaves me even more alone." Limitations may be inevitable, but they do not necessarily limit what you feel and need.

I want to help you see that, through our relationship, you can learn not just about what you don't have, or never had, but what you DO have. I want our relationship to eventually free you, not bind you into one of dependent vulnerability. Don't you see that you are not alone? You have made a remarkable step toward saying to me that you want and need me in a way that overwhelms you, in a way where other people in your life have failed you.

I am so terribly sorry that I didn't pick up on the dilemma that has been tearing at you—wanting not to need or care, and yet needing and caring so profoundly that you are more scared than words can say. I've told you all along that I will screw up, and I did. I will not make excuses, but point out that now we can talk about how we can up the odds of it not happening again. However, it will, and you will be disappointed in me. Somehow, I have to help you tell me, and not carry it all alone, and not have to leave us because of it. Definitely not leave us, because this relationship has that limitless possibility of being able to discuss and work out ANYTHING.

Your expectations and the neediness you are so in touch with now must be very, very scary. People have often failed you, set you up and left you, and so your reaction is not only understandable, but rational, given the circumstances of your life. You want to self-protect. You want to stop feeling that I matter as much as I do. But, for me, I want the opposite. We are (you and I), so to speak, a way to practice relationships. We will explore feelings and figure things out, and discuss them, and probably make mistakes, and discuss them again, and on, and on, and on.

I would like to continue talking about this during our next appointment. I hope that I can help you tolerate whatever you're experiencing so that some day, you will recognize your gifts, and the potential that exists for many incredible relationships in your future. Thank you, Terry.

Cali

CHAPTER 15

One Hundred Percent

October 2000

Naked in my thoughts, I stepped back through the door of Dr. Joseph's office. It was Monday morning and I could see the printouts of our e-mails lying on the table next to her chair. Cushioning the onslaught of my discomfort, Cali proceeded gently.

"How are you feeling?" she began.

"Embarrassed and vulnerable," I replied.

"Why?" she asked.

"Isn't it obvious?" I asked, immediately realizing the purposefulness of the e-mails' conspicuous location.

"I don't want to make any assumptions. I want to know what *you* are thinking."

"It's what I wrote. You know already," I replied.

"I know what you wrote, but I want to talk about it until we understand it more," Cali continued.

Once again, unveiled by shades of emotion across my face, I could feel my body stiffen with anxiety.

"Why are you so anxious?" Cali asked.

I shrugged my shoulders. My heart was threatening to burst right out of my chest. Writing was a helpful addition to our work, but Cali was not going to back-up and allow it to replace talking.

"Tell me, Terry. What's up?" she urged.

"I don't want to go through everything I wrote, again," I sighed. "The bottom line is that I just don't want to need you."

"It's too late, Terry. *This relationship happened,*" Cali declared.

This relatively simple statement managed to become a cornerstone in understanding our work together. I desperately wanted to cut off my feelings. But, like it or not, Dr. Joseph was right. *It was too late.* I no longer had the choice.

"But I can't allow myself to feel this way about you. This is business, not personal," I explained, struggling to repress the WP's *everything bagel* sensation that kept creeping back over me.

"You're right, Terry. This relationship is *100 percent business. But, it is also 100 percent personal.* Things aren't black or white. It doesn't have to be either/or."

I was breathless. I had been fighting against the existence of personal feelings, because, among other vulnerabilities, I presumed that such emotions were forbidden in the therapeutic setting—as though I really could have chosen what to feel about her at that point. "*100 percent business and 100 percent personal*"—they were words I would never forget.

"So, how do I prepare myself for losing you?" I asked. "It's a set-up for me to feel too much pain."

"Why do you think you will lose me?"

"Because, once therapy ends I won't have any contact with you. I don't know your telephone number, or where you live," I replied.

"Those boundaries will never preclude us from continuing our relationship. Even if I moved to China, you would always remain a part of my life. It wouldn't be dependent on your having my home telephone number or address," she said.

"Yes, it would," I argued. "Not having that information is what keeps me from being an insider," I explained.

"What's an insider?" Cali asked, keying in on the significance of the concept.

"It's belonging, or feeling connected to the people you are with, instead of being a visitor. It's being liked, loved or accepted by people—not just an outsider who is present in the periphery of the crowd," I explained.

The deceivingly complex notion of what it meant for me to be an "insider" was a revelation that would later prove to influence my understanding of all of the relationships in my life. I hadn't the slightest idea at the time, but this rather innocuous comment would mark the beginning of what would become months of profound self-discoveries.

"Is feeling like an outsider familiar to you?" Cali asked.

"Yes," I replied, in spite of my aversion to questions resembling textbook, therapeutic rhetoric.

"When else have you felt that way?"

"I've had to manage that feeling for a majority of my life.

I think it started when I was in my teens. Mostly, I was a loner. That's why losing Kurt felt so much worse than anyone realizes. Being with him was the first time I felt like an insider. I was filled up, and I belonged. I never thought I would have to feel like an outsider again," I explained.

"Do you remember feeling that way before your teens?"

"Yeah, I suppose when I was in grade school," I answered.

"What is the earliest time in your life you remember feeling like an outsider?"

I could feel the nausea rolling around in my stomach, as I searched through the visions of childhood loneliness that began to race through my mind.

"Maybe 10 years old. Or, somewhere around the fourth grade," I guessed, relying on the house I lived in as the best gauge of time.

"Ah. *10 years old*, again," Cali teasingly remarked. "Did pretending that feeling like an outsider *didn't* matter to you, make it bother you any less?" she asked.

"No," I answered, heading off the routine dialogue that inevitably disproved my former "avoid it so it won't bother me" philosophy.

"You should have a plaque that says, '*I don't want it to matter*' nailed above the front door of your house. Do you realize this is your motto?" Cali asked. I hadn't really thought about it before. "What's the price you pay for that? You won't stop needing what matters to you. Trying to manage the struggle alone by not talking about it will only make those feelings that much more difficult to deal with."

"But, either way, my feelings *are* difficult to deal with. Having you matter so much makes the boundaries feel even more intolerable every time I leave here," I said.

"We both have to face restrictions in each other's lives, but they are there for a reason, Terry. Our relationship is very unique, and while you may think that these limits exclude you, they actually *give* you something that is *very* different from what you experience with others," Cali explained.

"I don't understand how that's possible."

"Do you talk to your friends the same way that you do here?" Cali asked.

"No," I replied.

"Do any of your friends listen to you like I do?"

"No."

"Do you think I talk with my friends, family or the other people in my personal life like I do with you?"

"I don't know. It's the way you think, isn't it?" I asked.

"No, Terry. This is not the way I interact with people outside the office. My attention is entirely different here. The conversations you and I have are never about me, or my needs. When we sit here together, it's about *you*. The focus is to find ways to help *you*. Do you understand the difference?" Cali asked

"Yeah," I reluctantly replied.

"What else do you think is different about our relationship?" Cali continued. As always, she was going to force me to reason through every answer.

"I suppose the privacy. I know that whatever I say will remain confidential. And I don't have to worry about being selfish, or over burdening you," I strained. As difficult as it was to admit, I had never thought about the value of the boundaries. Yet, the logic still offered me no relief. The more sensible the limitations became, the more my uneasiness grew over having to continue enduring her absence between sessions.

"Yes, that's true. You can tell me *anything*, and I will never pass judgment on you. There is *nothing* you could say to me that would make me not like you," she added. "Can you see how important it is to preserve the limits?"

"But, I still have to deal with feeling like an outsider. Once I leave here, I don't have access to you, and I have to repeatedly make the adjustments from one appointment to the next," I explained, noticing the evolvement of my comfort level at being forthright about my feelings toward Dr. Joseph.

"But you *do* have access to me. I carry a pager, and you can call my service. In fact, that is another very unique difference," Cali pointed out. "Terry, I'm not hiding behind 'professional boundaries.' I know this is difficult for you. Some limitations can be fluid over time, but it's very important that we always figure out what would be most helpful to you first," Cali explained.

"It would be helpful if I could feel like an insider."

"But, you *are* an insider, Terry. The question is, *what do you need from me in order to feel it?*" Cali asked, with a profound emphasis on the more central issue.

"I don't know," I squirmed. I could barely tolerate the vulnerability I felt when I *wrote* about how much I needed her. Stomaching the exposure of *telling* her WHAT I needed from her, out loud, to her face was unbearable.

"Is it that you don't know, or is it that you don't want to say?" she perceptively asked.

"I don't want to say," I admitted, beginning to feel the monotony of my response.

"Why not?" Cali prodded.

"Because, I feel too vulnerable."

"What can I do to help you? How can I make it more comfortable for you to say what you need from me?"

"I don't know."

"Do you think you could write to me again?" she asked.

"Yeah, I suppose so," I replied, thankful for the respite of her offer.

"Please give it a try, Terry. See what you can do, okay?" Cali suggested.

"I'll try," I agreed.

The subtle benefits of the therapeutic process were unfolding. I thought we were in the midst of discussing an impossible predicament. But, Cali had found a way to slowly pry me away from the solitude and inflexibility of my thoughts. For the very first time during the months I struggled alone in confusion, she had found an avenue for me to begin openly admitting to my feelings. Despite my initial embarrassment and protests, I had begun to speak.

11:30 P.M.

Cali,

I once told you that what I needed was for YOU to want something, but I was too confused, and then embarrassed, to say what that "something" was. Well, what I needed (or, what I need) was for YOU to want me to be an insider (in the way I see it). I know you don't share my feelings. And I know that as long as there are restrictions (time limits, access by telephone, etc.), I will continue to feel on the outside of your life.

But, now you've asked me, SPECIFICALLY, what I need FROM you to FEEL like an insider, and I still cannot arrive at an answer. I think that is a question that warrants repeating until I can answer it and so, despite the discomfort, in an odd way I'm glad you persist.

However, I think the question I keep asking myself may be more helpful: if I could have you say or do anything in the universe that I wanted, realistic or not, what is it that you could do or say that would make me feel better, reassured, or less afraid? I guess it would be for YOU to say the following:

"Terry, I know it's unconventional for this business, codes of conduct, and so forth, but this relationship is different, and all that doesn't really matter in this unique situation. You don't have to page me to talk to me, or to see me, and you don't have to remain on the outside of my life, with these 'professional' walls up. Boundaries can change and I want them to, in time, if it's comfortable. I'd love to be your friend, or mentor, and look after you. I won't always keep these walls up."

I am so confused. So UNBELIEVABLY confused. I do not want to feel this way, yet I do. So, what are the risks of telling you all of this? That I'll come in and hear you confirm that there has to be, and always will be, boundaries. Or, that I won't be able to come in, because I need to shut these needs and wants off.

I can't think of any other options—not surprising to you, I am sure. I hope you know how frighteningly dependent I am on you and this process to help me find a way to end this dilemma. Obviously, I'm hoping for other options and I think that's why I'm writing this rather than fleeing in the other direction.

See what you get when you ask me to be honest? This is about as open as I can be with anyone. But, I will remain committed to not filtering my thoughts and feelings. I'll spend the next few days regretting sending this, but what the hell, someone I trust once told me that it would be worth it to face my feelings rather than run from them.

Terry

8:11 A.M.

Terry,

So now we start to explore together that very person that has been in hiding since almost forever. You see boundaries as barriers to that exploration. I see them as entrances, as beginnings. I told you a while ago, and I will tell you again, and again, and again, until you believe it, until you believe me, that everything is open to discussion. There is nothing, NOTHING, that we cannot figure out. And there are always options as long as we continue to talk. And I have many examples of this from our work together.

You and I both know that we have often begun with an incredibly difficult issue, one that creates for you tremendous anxiety and terror. Slowly, we face it together, and discuss it, and look at it, and then look at it again (for you, at times, ad nauseam). We figure it out, leave it, come back and look at it some more. It changes shape, and color, and it takes new forms. Through the talking, we see it in a new way, and we end up amazed, and that much closer to an understanding. This is our evolving relationship, and if we look back to where we were, and then to where we are now, we can both experience the true wonder of it all, and the incredible possibilities for where it will and can go. We have to figure it out, together, and while you may not, I have all the faith we need, to know that we can.

You talk of me having options that you don't have, but I think you have failed to pay attention to the options YOU have that I don't have. And so we come to some "dis-equality" and at times, for both of us, this will be challenging. And once again, hopefully, we can talk about when we experience this, and how our relationship will evolve and continue to take on a new and different meaning.

So, you ask, what are the risks? Oh Terry, the risks are great—I know that. And I have told you again and again that I will fail you in unknowing ways and that I need you to talk to me, to tell me, and to trust in the unique "us" and mostly to trust in yourself and your worth. I appreciate how incredibly intense this is for you. But I want to help you understand that the risks are so much greater if you run—so much greater if you continue to shut off and keep yourself so hidden that your gifts are never experienced by anybody else.

I see what I get when I ask you to be honest. I see limitless potential. And by the way, that someone whom you trust—you know, the one that told you it would be worth it to face it all rather than run—her advice is very, very good. I would take it, and hold on to her, and go with it.

Cali

CHAPTER 16

Relationships Happen

October 2000

All the blood had already rushed to my head and I hadn't
even taken a seat yet. Dr. Joseph's office was a place with no
pretenses. Motionless, I waited for her to start in with some
rapid-fire questions, hoping I could spend the time swallowing
my anxiety with monosyllabic responses. Instead, she just sat
there, waiting for me to take the lead.

"What's up?" Cali asked a few moments later.

"What do you mean?" I asked. Cali seemed so calm. My
organs, on the other hand, were busy relocating themselves all
over the inside of my body.

"I'm not going to do your work for you, Terry," she replied.

A couple of things immediately became clear. This was my
session, not hers. I was the one paying to be there, and I was
the one who had something to lose if the time was not made
useful. Despite the difficulty I had in producing the words,
I realized she could far outlast me in a staring contest and at
some point, I was going to have to start things off.

"Do you feel like you have to manage things differently
because of what I've told you?" I asked. I was terrified that the
intensity of the feelings in my e-mails was going to cause Dr.
Joseph to back away.

"What do you mean?" she asked.

Almost muted by acute anxiety, I attempted to explain. "I don't want you to protect me from feeling rejection. If you are looking for a way out, I would rather know up front than be placated."

"Now do you understand why it's so important to wait and see where your thoughts go? It's so much more useful than discussing whatever I'm thinking," Cali began. I couldn't help but agree that addressing this fear was most pressing.

"Terry, telling me how you feel about me did not overwhelm or scare me. Backing away hadn't even entered my mind, and I don't feel like I have to manage you. I'm really glad you asked me this question. This is what I mean about the importance of talking. If I know what you're concerned about, we have the opportunity to discuss it. In fact, I'm glad you're struggling with this dilemma about caring too much. You see, I want you to care *even more*, not less."

More rather than less? I never imagined that would be her response. Had I not asked the question, I would have put myself under enormous pressure to keep my feelings in check. I was relieved to know that Cali wasn't juggling her feelings, or trying to figure out how to manage me. Yet, I still could not give myself license to feel, as long as I continued to stare at the imbalance between us.

"What did you mean by 'dis-equality'?" I asked, referring to her e-mail.

"I meant that there are two sides to this relationship, and to some extent, both of us face limitations with each other. I could no more come into your life uninvited than you could into mine," Cali answered.

"Sure you could. And, I don't see how you are limited at all. You can contact me, but I cannot contact you. You know my home number, but I don't know yours. You know where I live, but I don't know your address. You know who my family and friends are, and what I am doing when I'm not here. You can contact me anytime," I protested.

"Terry, I may have that information, but that doesn't mean I could ever pull into your driveway, or show up at your house unannounced. And, there are many reasons for preserving the disparities. We are here for *you*, not for *me*. It would not be helpful if we talked about my feelings or my life, and what I'm doing outside the office," Cali said.

"I understand that the process is about me. But, regardless of the purpose, the limits are unilateral—they still only apply to me," I said.

"Have you ever thought about the limits I must tolerate, from my side of this relationship?" Cali asked.

"Like what?" I was dumbfounded.

"When you walk out of here, I am never certain that you are coming back. You could call me, or not call me, and terminate therapy at any time, and there is nothing I could do to force you to continue seeing me. I could lose you, you could leave, and I would have to accept your decision," she finished.

"But, you *could* terminate treatment just as easily as me. And, you *could* contact me," I argued. "You say that you couldn't come into my life uninvited. But the truth is, not only would I have no problem with it, I've wished for it on countless occasions," I confessed.

"Just because I know your address, or because it's something you wish for, doesn't mean I could do so. We don't have that kind of relationship, Terry. It just doesn't work," she responded. "Sometimes, patients invite me to their parties. But I cannot go. The relationships are very different, and it gets very confusing. For example, I recently paid a condolence call to a patient's house. I don't regret going because his loss was profound. People made comments like, 'so you're the one that knows everything,' and it was awkward. I saw the patient in his own personal environment. It became more of an observation. Crossing boundaries is very complicated."

"I understand. But, I'm not asking you to come to my parties. It's the absences in between our appointments that I just can't deal with. In fact, it actually makes coming in here feel worse," I said.

"What do you mean?" Cali asked, looking intrigued.

"I know you are going to think this is all about my childhood after I say this, but it's *not*. It just reminds me of what I dealt with when I was growing up. My parents got divorced when I was three. They constantly fought over custody. The judge's rulings were very strict. My father only had visitation rights every other weekend. He was not allowed to contact me in between visits. No phone calls, no school activities—nothing. I missed him terribly between visits. But, even though I looked forward to our next visit, by the time that weekend arrived, there was a part of me that didn't want to see him. And then, there was a part of me that didn't want to be at my mother's house after he dropped me off. I dreaded having to repeatedly make the adjustments. It would take days for the pain to subside, and I hated having to live in that cycle," I explained.

"Geez, Terry, now you are doing the work. Do you see the association you've made? I can only imagine how you must have felt when you were a little girl. But, the difference here is that you are now an adult. You don't have to *live with* anything. You can make your own choices. Most importantly, you have the ability to *talk* about what you need, and then go after it. I don't expect you to live each day tolerating how you are feeling now. But, I do expect that we will be able to figure out a way for you to feel better. We may not know how that will happen right now, but we've both been here before."

"When have we been here before?" I asked, still digesting the pivotal difference between the silent subordination of my childhood, and the ability to talk about things as an adult. It was the *very first* crack I felt in my expectation that I was doomed to live in the cycle of my predicament.

"We've disagreed about a number of things that never seemed resolvable to you. But, when we talked them out, we developed different understandings, and we were able to find compromises, so that we could both feel more comfortable," Cali answered.

"Like what?" I asked. My head was whirling with too many new perspectives for me to put it all together at the moment.

"We were able to accomplish this with the dilemma we faced over hospitalization, and with the difficulties about the drugs," Cali pointed out.

"But, this is different," I replied with predictable skepticism. "It's impossible, because although I really do understand the reasons behind preserving the limits, they are the very boundaries that perpetuate the pain of being an outsider. This time *I know* I'm stuck where I am. I know it's not something we can work out," I contended.

"You don't know that until you first figure out exactly what it is that you need, and then ask for it."

"You don't understand," I said, exasperated.

"Yes, I do. In fact, I understand more than you realize. Something just became clearer to me. This is what I mean about the talking, Terry. Sometimes it takes going over and over things before something shifts."

"I started dating my husband when I was in graduate school," Cali continued to explain. "We went to different schools and because of the distance I could only see him on some weekends. I missed him terribly when we were apart. It got to the point where I could only enjoy Friday nights with him because I was so preoccupied with the dread of his leaving on Sunday that I sabotaged the whole weekend. I think this is what you may be experiencing," Cali suggested.

"So, you see? You understand what I'm going through, and why it's *not* resolvable. Even if I asked for what I want, I wouldn't be able to get it," I responded.

"You're right. I do understand. But you're wrong about not being able to work it out. Just as I found with my situation, as you feel differently about yourself and your life, the adjustments will become less difficult. There is no question in my mind that if we continue to talk about this, we will find ways to help you feel more comfortable. It does not have to be all or nothing. Maybe we can find ways to respect the limitations, and still help bridge the gap to make the absences more tolerable. I think the e-mails are helping, aren't they?"

"Yeah," I replied. I just wanted out. That's all I could feel. I hated wishing that I could stay there. I hated wanting to make a run for it. All I could think about from the beginning of the appointment was the end, when I would have to leave and face another few days of struggling without her presence.

"So, let's keep the e-mails going as you need to. And I really want you to think about something. I want you to think about whether you would really want to trade our relationship for the kind of relationship you have with others. The limits are what enable us to do this work, and we will not be able to continue this form of a relationship without them. I want you to begin to understand that the boundaries don't limit us. They give us *limitless* possibilities," Cali explained.

I wished I could run and not look back, but I cared too much to move. I was fighting my feelings, but Cali was relentless. *Any* opportunity to tap into *any* emotion, particularly one of connectedness, provided Dr. Joseph with a welcomed reprieve from the dangers of my apathy. All I could think about was my motto. I desperately wanted to make her not matter. However, what no longer mattered was my ability to choose what I did and did not want to feel. The relationship had happened.

CHAPTER 17

Selfish Help

November 2000

I discretely glanced around the bookstore before reaching toward the shelf. No one was in sight. My fingers took hold of the binding, and as I clenched the tiny, hardcover book tight to my chest, I wandered over to a seat in the most remote corner of the store. *Final Departure*, an instruction book for assisted suicides. Noting the irony of the soothing hum of Christmas carols playing overhead, I skimmed the contents and quickly located what I was looking for.

Many evenings had been spent breezing through the scores of books designed for the bereaved, and those on how to overcome the hazards of depression. Although the resources were plentiful, I was well beyond the help of the written word. Understandably, the self-help section did not offer the pharmaceutical formulas necessary to end one's life. I had read through enough articles during Kurt's illness to know that any recipes for painless certainty were going to be buried in the books intended for the terminally ill.

The disclosure of my feelings of attachment to Dr. Joseph had backfired on me. Despite her repeated assurances otherwise, I refused to believe that we could resolve the agony of my loneliness in between appointments. I was torn between wanting Cali to take care of me, and pulling away from her so that I could end what I believed was my fated misery. The irreversibility of my decision was of little consequence as I was drawn to the more immediate relief of death as my inevitable solution. I began to prepare myself with the requisite information on how to proceed whenever that moment would arrive.

Overall, I had kept my word to Dr. Joseph to remain straight. However, the repetitious exchanges of the key to my supply cabinet had become like an over worn yo-yo falling off its string. Every opportunity I had between promises was filled with barely controllable over-indulgence. It was just past the year mark since Kurt's death, and my private world of substances had escalated into an unrelenting routine.

The day often began with opening my eyes to the carpet of the living room floor somewhere around noontime—marking the end of a six to twelve hour semi-coma. I spent what remained of my afternoon recovering from the assault, and attempting to reconstruct the previous evening. Clues often included a toppled over prescription vial, an empty bottle of wine, or a martini glass lying next to my "bed." Slips of paper scribbled with barely legible words and phrases were my only reminders of whatever telephone conversations had taken place. Typically, I only had a vague memory, if *any* at all, of the calls. The cycle continued with the arrival of darkness, wherein I recommenced the obliteration until I collapsed back into unconsciousness. I had no fear of a potential overdose. In fact, I was inviting it.

Somewhere in between black outs, I managed to squeeze in a social engagement or two. Yet the strain of keeping up appearances in my personal life drove me further into the abyss. I was juggling my appointments, and the intermittent agreements with Dr. Joseph, but we were both losing the battle against the drugs. I continued to stubbornly refuse any suggestion to consider anti-depressant medication—a futile alternative unless I agreed to a concomitant sobriety, anyway. My commitment to treatment was erratic, and the entryway to Cali's office had become a revolving door. One day I was dedicated, and the next I was announcing that I could no longer return to therapy. Even when I was showing up for sessions, I was becoming increasingly silent and unreachable.

Short of eliminating every necessary boundary line between a therapist and patient, Dr. Joseph was willing to consider anything that would help ease my discomfort over having to adjust to her absence. She even provided me with her direct pager number so that I would not have to go through her service in order to contact her. Yet, despite her efforts to persuade me that I was in fact an insider, I simply could not feel it through the painful isolation of my weekends. Our e-mails continued through what had become the almost daily struggle to get from one appointment to the next. Cali fought to instill even the slightest hope that my despair was not permanent as long as we continued to talk. Nevertheless, the unyielding grip of depression had me by the throat, and I could barely embrace the notion that the core of my feelings would ever change.

It took some time before I was able to recognize the self-defeating cycle of my thought process. I had justified my excessive use of substances as a safeguard that numbed me away from the temptation of suicide. However, it was that very intoxication that exacerbated my depression by scrambling every neuron in my brain. Contrary to what I believed, the drugs and alcohol were causing me to think *more* about ending my life, not *less*. If for no other reason, the fact that I was hiding in the corner of a bookstore with a stack of medical reference books in front of me was proof positive of that reality.

My focus turned back to the table of contents. The first few pages were riddled with legal disclaimers and overstated warnings against the misuse of the author's advice.

The boldfaced messages suggested that anyone reviewing the material for purposes of ending their own life, due to depression, immediately put the book down. It urged those people to seek counseling, consider hospitalization, anti-depressant medication, or enlist the help of family members. Undoubtedly, the book was written solely to help the terminally ill end their suffering, not to aid otherwise healthy people who were seeking death as a means to end their emotional anguish. However, I had irrationally concluded that I was in fact putting an end to my own "terminal illness"—my destined life of intolerable misery, regardless of the help I sought. I knew that if I was going to open that door, I was going to walk through it without turning back. There would be no attempts. I remained committed to my distorted objective to achieve a "successful suicide"—in retrospect, quite the oxymoron.

A small child bumped against my knee and jolted my attention away from the self-consuming world I had entered. I set the book down on my leg, and watched as he giggled past me, chased affectionately away by his mother. The bookstore had become crowded and filled with the buzz of holiday shopping. I glanced around, imagining what it would be like to be anyone—to be *any* single person other than me.

From where I sat, I could see several people searching through the shelves of the travel section. I wondered if they were planning a family trip, and romanticized about what choices they were considering. Or, were they by themselves, looking for a way to escape the darkness of the holiday season, and ease their loneliness?

I turned towards the rows piled infinitely high with hundreds of self-help and motivational books. I imagined the variations of suffering that led people down those aisles. Widows looking for a way to cope with their loss or survivors of child abuse needing the support offered by the accounts of those with similar experiences. Maybe they had been sent by a terminally-ill loved one, or spouse, and were struggling through the dilemma of seeking the very assistance intended to be provided by the book draped over my knee. Maybe there was even someone just like me, looking at suicide as a way out after hopelessly concluding that the "self-help" section no longer applied to them.

I proceeded through the materials until I located the pertinent chapter containing ingredient charts of various lethal combinations. I hadn't braced myself for the chilling recommendations that were to follow—a very particularized process that required step-by-step preparations. As I continued to read through the pages, I was overcome with the guilt of my selfishness, and despised myself for my inability to appreciate and embrace my life.

I thought about the circumstances for which the book was designed, and the turmoil of those, such as Kurt, who were wholly dependent on others because they were too debilitated to execute a plan. I thought about the thousands of terminally-ill people who would have traded places with me in a second. They were fighting for their lives, and would have given anything for a second chance, while I was contemplating throwing away a physically healthy body.

Finally, I had read enough to put the book down and rethink my intentions. I felt afraid, alone, and trapped in my confusion. I thought about the work I had done with Dr. Joseph and the mockery I would be making of all that I had learned from the therapeutic process. I thought about the impact I would have on the people in my life when they heard the news of my death. I struggled to hold onto the hope that other feelings were possible if I could just stay the course. I grappled with the selfishness of my actions just by virtue of even looking at the book. Dr. Joseph had trusted me. I had given her my word that I would call her if I seriously began to consider an attempt. But, the wall I had built had two sides. She could not get in and I could not get out. I felt the gnawing onslaught of all sorts of potential, personal repercussions.

With the debate still screaming inside of me, I waited in the long line of shoppers until I reached the cash register. Still unresolved, I handed the book to the cashier, and watched her tally up the final amount due. I then made my payment with the currency of betrayal.

CHAPTER 18

The Red Pen

November 2000

The distortion of time felt like the melting clocks on a Salvador Dali painting. I could not recall a lengthier weekend. Alone in my thoughts, staring down the barrel of my drug cocktail, I bore a new empathy for the torturous pace of solitary confinement. Thanksgiving had passed, but my life had not gone along with it. Logic had become a stranger, and somehow, I was still treading the surface of a drowning current. I restored the bottle of Percocets to my drug cabinet as my fears managed to drive me back to the telephone to call Dr. Joseph.

"I really need to come in and talk to you," I began. For reasons still unknown to me, I had failed miserably at my attempts to make Cali not matter and proceed with my plan to terminate therapy and end my life.

"Do you want to come in tomorrow?" she asked.

"Yes," I answered. We booked an appointment for the following morning. Relieved from the exhaustion of my suicidal debate, I collapsed into the first sleep I had since I last walked out of her office.

Sitting across from Dr. Joseph, I continued to debate silently the usefulness of full disclosure. I didn't have the courage to tell her how close I had come, but I was desperate to alleviate the weight of my life or death struggle. While I still didn't want to be in her office, there was no place I would rather have been.

"Why did you need to come in?" Cali began.

"Because, I spent the entire weekend wanting to die, and I couldn't make you not matter," I answered.

"What do you mean?"

"I thought about overdosing, about taking everything," I confessed, omitting the particulars.

"So, *you were going to break your promises to me?*" Cali's voice rose with anger.

"No, that's why I called."

"I'm so glad you called, Terry. But, we need to talk about trust again. If I have to worry that you're going to break your promises to me, how can we do this work?"

I knew the rules.

"I don't know. I've just been feeling desperate to find a way to stop feeling like this," I said, with empty eyes that screamed of the black hole I was in.

"Terry, I need to insist that you give me a relative's telephone number," Cali demanded.

"Why?" I pretended not to know, but her fear of my potential, unexplained failure to appear was the obvious answer.

Dr. Joseph handed me a piece of paper and a pen. Trying to ignore the intended symbolism of the color, I wrote down the telephone number in red ink and handed it back to her.

"I need you to promise me again, Terry. I need to know that you will not get high, and that you will keep yourself safe," Cali persisted.

"Okay," I whispered, looking down at the floor.

"I want you to look me in the eyes and say it."

"I promise," I sighed, barely able to glance above my neck as I struggled with the fear of a reconfirmed commitment to stay alive.

"Not good enough, Terry. I want you to look at me and say the whole thing," Cali demanded, making my dentist's job of pulling teeth look amateur.

"*Okay*, I promise I will not get high, and that I will keep myself safe."

"Will you consider taking some medication that will help you feel better, until we can figure this out?" Cali asked with the return of compassion in her voice.

"No. We've already gone over this, Cali," I obstinately replied.

"Yes, I know. But, I want to go over it again. I want to understand why you are still refusing to do something that will help you."

"Because, I don't want to take anything that will make me feel artificial," I irritably repeated for what felt like the one-hundredth time.

"Terry, medication will *not* change who you are. It will help to make the bottom less deep. There are a lot of medications to choose from, and I have an excellent psycho-pharm doctor to refer you to. Medication won't replace therapy, and we'll need to continue to do this work. But in the meantime, it will be a tool to help you feel less depressed," Cali urged.

"No, Cali, I won't take anything."

"I don't understand. Why won't you just *try* something? You can stop anytime you want if you don't like how you are feeling. So what do you have to lose?"

"I don't want to talk about it anymore," I retorted.

"Are you angry?" Cali asked.

"No, I'm just *not* going to take anti-depressants. I'm not going to do it," I answered, containing my irritation and hoping a calmer refusal would put an end to her persistence.

"What are you feeling?"

"Nothing. That's the point. I'm not interested in anything," I said.

"But, you're interested in this process," Cali reminded me. Coming to her office was just about the only thing I had a desire to do.

"Yes. But, I've never felt so alone, and I continue to agonize over the absences in between our appointments. And, I just don't want to care anymore," I hopelessly whined.

"Why don't you want to care, Terry? So you can go kill yourself more easily? I won't be a part of that, and I won't be a part of making things not matter to you," Cali emphatically declared.

170

We were both frustrated. Cali knew she was not reaching me, and I felt like I was not reaching her—or anything in life for that matter. We were embroiled in a true, psychological tug-of-war. She wanted me to consider anti-depressant medication, and to have faith that things could change to a more comfortable place—even with the limitations inherent to our relationship. I wanted her to understand my desire to die, and the importance of removing some of the boundaries in order to end the suffering I felt in between sessions. We continued to talk and debate the issues ad nauseam, but depression was suffocating me. As time went on, I was less and less able to speak through my metastasizing, apathetic stupor. Writing had remained the most effective way for me to communicate. E-mails soon became an inextricable component of salvaging our communications, and my last attempts to keep myself afloat.

12:13 A.M.

Dear Cali,

After partially decompressing, I was wondering after I left yesterday if our meeting was a waste of time. It almost goes without saying that our talk seemed a bit less than fluid. Is this what you were referring to when you said there would be times when I would be pissed off?

Anyway, I'm thinking about compromises and all the rest of the things we've been discussing. My ongoing efforts to keep my promises, as well as tolerate the discomfort of the adjustments in between sessions, (without any compromises from your end) are becoming nearly impossible to maintain. Maybe I've missed something, but it seems that I'm not able to see or feel what steps have been made, or are being made, toward

*making any of this easier, or more tolerable on my end. I am
wondering if you are now in a place where it is this way or no
way.*

*You asked me why I didn't tell you what was going on that
led up to my suicidal debate during Thanksgiving weekend.
I explained a number of reasons why I felt I couldn't tell you
about it. You then told me that all I needed to say was, "I'm
not getting what I want or need, and I feel like dying," and
how that could've led to a discussion of how to improve the
situation. It seemed like such an obvious suggestion, but until
that moment, it had never occurred to me that it could be as
simple as that. So, rather than not saying the simple things, I
am writing this to you. I haven't had the greatest night, and
I've been in such a black hole. Not good so far.*

Terry

10:03 P.M.

Dear Terry,

*You write of "partially decompressing" after our last
appointment. Since you denied feeling angry during
the session, I'm left wondering what emotion you were
decompressing from. If you were indeed angry, I wonder why
you can't discuss it while you are sitting with me. Please think
about this, okay? I want to talk to you about it when we are
together.*

*We are in the midst of very, very hard stuff, Terry. We are
fighting to make you feel like living is worthwhile. When you
obsess on the question of being alive versus being dead, you
don't feel anything but this hopeless sense of eternal pain. You*

may not agree with me that feeling angry or sad is better than feeling pain, but there is method to this madness. The more you get behind the pain, the more you have a range of emotions, and the more possibility you have to make some room for the good stuff, like joy, excitement, and interest in things.

You are stuck in an obsessive and endless battle with yourself. I am trying desperately to get in there, to help you leave it, and instead, help you battle the demons that got you there in the first place. If you are going to fight, then fight the real enemies.

You will be mad at me, because you are holding on with all your might to what is familiar and long standing. And, I'm fighting to pry your hold on that obsessive battle that so overwhelmingly occupies your time and mind. That's okay, Terry. I would rather you be mad at me than at yourself and the situation you have been in for so long.

You can't see the steps that are being made toward making things easier because you are in terrible pain and filled with so many feelings that you are fighting to keep out of consciousness. I know it's almost intolerable, but it isn't this work that is so intolerable. It is the place you are in.

You came to me over a year ago. You were numb, miserable, and needed direction through a tunnel that would show you some light. You have been in the dark so long, with only some minor breaks. You have to allow yourself time to feel and experience more than you have before. I know this sounds like psychobabble to you. It isn't. We have to find a way to put the life/death battle aside, at least some of the time, so that we can battle your history and make the future better than your past.

I know you feel that you are not getting what you want but it is unfair, if I may use that term, to say that I'm suggesting that it's my way or no way. I know it's difficult for you to see

*the compromises I've made to help you, the steps forward
I've made in order to be more available and open to you, and
the things you need. While it may not FEEL like much, it is
different than saying I haven't compromised, or moved from
some past place. And, without a doubt I must compromise
even more. Our relationship will continue to be fluid. I will
constantly try to understand more of what you need, and what
will help you. It took you 35 years to get to where you are. You
bring the demons with you. Please, don't let the demons kill
you.*

*I know that you suffer each and every separation. But you
HAVE gotten through them, and you must acknowledge this.
The work is so hard, but it has to be done. You have to feel
ALL the feelings. Even the crummy ones. It is better than the
obsessive battle you have waged for decades.*

*The ride ahead is a rough one, Terry. But you won't be alone
this time. That is my promise to you.*

Cali

Despite repeated impasses, I struggled to keep every
appointment during the remaining weeks before Christmas.
Our e-mails continued to supplement our efforts to reach
compromises and better understandings. While clearly stating
her preference was to do the work in person, Dr. Joseph
was willing to consider any alternative short of letting me
terminate therapy. She offered to schedule appointments on the
telephone, or to work through e-mails if coming into the office
was too much to tolerate. If the intensity of our work was too
much for me, she suggested fewer sessions, or tempering the
content of our talks in order to "turn down the volume" for a

while. However, regardless of the steps that could have been taken, I had put up one apathetic roadblock after another.

Christmas arrived in no time, and our last appointment before the holiday became a silent dance. Dr. Joseph was going to be out of the country on vacation for one week. She strove to alleviate the absence with as much access to help as possible. She left me the name and number of a therapist that would be covering for her during her time away. She encouraged me to write and promised we would discuss anything I was feeling when she returned.

We scheduled an appointment for January 3rd and I left her office under the guise of being somewhat reassured. Yet, lethargy had made it increasingly impossible for Cali to read me. She was looking into my deadened eyes. I was looking at a dead end. It would be a long while before there was any meeting of the minds. Despite almost Herculean efforts, I headed into the week with no idea whether or not I was going to ever see the New Year. I once read that sometimes it takes staring death right in the eye before you can come out of a suicidal debate. Until I faced that moment, somehow, I knew that nothing was going to be enough.

CHAPTER 19

The Anomaly

December 27, 2000

My body landed like an oak tree after receiving the final chop of a lumberjack's swing. Except for my cheek smashing against the floor, I have no recollection of first opening my eyes. The tile of the bathroom floor was the first thing I saw. I was completely anesthetized, fully incapable of feeling anything except the weight of my body as it pounded the breath right out of me. A corpse with a pulse. Reconstructing my memory began with my piecing together the sporadic moments of consciousness that followed.

Judging from my body's slam against the tile, my guess was that I had traveled from the bed to the adjoining bathroom with the incoherence of the walking dead. Contrary to the natural order of evolution from infancy to old age, this was my birth from death to life, an excruciating re-entry into existence.

At some point, I attempted to pull myself up from the floor. Gravity was not cooperative. I vaguely recall landing face first again, and then some sort of military crawl across the floor and again just lying there, feeling heavy—a heap of flesh that was taking up space, not even ambulatory enough to take my face off the floor.

Gradually, the faintest communication between my mind and my senses began to emerge, as I became aware of my transfixion on an object. Sometime later, I identified the focus of my timelessly blank stare. It was my foot. I began to process a connection between the blood on the floor and the gash on my toe, cut open after I had bumped a framed photograph off the wall.

Resembling those of a newborn infant, my movements originated from instinct rather than stream of thought. I managed to climb into a seated position against the bathroom wall. Although I had yet to even comprehend my own existence, my brain somehow directed me to retrieve a bandage from the cabinet beneath the sink. However, my arms were like foreign mechanisms that no longer belonged to me. My hands blindly missed the drawer and my fingers clumsily groped for the knob, making the execution of the task impossible. Ultimately, I had to abandon my efforts until my mind and body could re-learn cooperation.

Seconds, minutes, or perhaps hours later, I began to discern the shocking reality. Contrary to the laws of science, I was still alive, seated on the bathroom floor a few feet from my bed— an anatomical aberration that was nothing short of miraculous. One of my worst fears had become a reality. I had woken up from committing suicide.

After several attempts, I gripped the door handle and swayed into a standing position. The eyes reflected back in the bathroom mirror were barely recognizable; a complete stranger now occupied my body. The disconnection was the visual equivalent of touching my lip after receiving a dose of Novocain from the dentist—the motions of the physical world bearing almost no internal relationship to sensation.

I reached to turn the handle of the faucet for some water, but the uncontrollable twitching in my hands rendered them virtually nonfunctional—a symptom I later learned was attributable to the onset of liver failure. Scant images of what I had done on Christmas morning began to reassemble, and my stupor rapidly gave way to the terrifying possibility that I had sustained irreversible brain damage.

I was immediately torn by the dilemma over whether to finish the job. Apparently, even with the ingestion of enough drugs to kill an elephant, my body was not going to accept an overdose. Dominated by acute despair and still saturated with the massive invasion of narcotics and alcohol, I began to weigh the grisly details of my predicament. Depression did not beget rationality.

I concluded that the only remaining, "logical" course of action was to slit my wrists—an option with its own set of colossal complications. I dreaded the physical pain from repeatedly having to cut deep into my flesh, through muscle, tendons, and veins. Whether the spasms in my hands would enable me to hold a razor blade with any precision was questionable. My efforts to minimize the gruesomeness of the scene when my body was discovered would become preposterous. And lastly, God forbid, I feared waking up from *that* attempt, relegated to a life with paralysis and extensive disability from severing the nerves to my hands. Any way I was capable of looking at it, I found myself living in an altogether new place in hell. I didn't know it then, but I had yet to learn the agony of being trapped in my new domicile. The downsides of proceeding ultimately won out, and I collapsed onto my bed.

Soaked with perspiration, I was soon awakened, shivering with the arrival of insufferable dry heaves. Numbness had transformed itself into merciless nausea and cramping throughout my digestive system. As my condition became exceedingly intolerable, I realized that it was in an altogether different league from a passing hangover, and that the worst was probably yet to come. I cautiously placed one foot in front of the other and unsteadily navigated my way into the kitchen to call my friend, Paul, for a ride to the hospital.

Ordinarily, I knew his phone number as well as my own, but I could not remember any of it. The convulsing of my hands caused me to repeatedly drop the phone to the floor. Unable to compute the sequence of numbers, I finally managed to press the button on the speed dial. A course of unforgivable deceit began as I explained that I had been waiting out the flu for a couple of days, I was not improving and thought it best to be taken to the emergency room. Although we had known each other for over 25 years, Paul had to ask to whom he was speaking. My speech sounded like it was playing from the last few seconds of a tape recorder just before the batteries ran out. My tongue felt as though it had been dipped in glue and produced a tone of voice that was unrecognizable even to me.

While I awaited Paul's arrival, terror began to engulf me. I remembered Dr. Joseph mentioning that people are rarely accorded the respect of personalized attention when they are brought to the emergency room after a suicide attempt. My panic spiraled into visions of being placed in restraints and being subjected to involuntary commitment if my actions were discovered.

I managed to hobble through each room, gather up the drugs I had not taken, and surreptitiously disperse them into various hiding places throughout the house. My equilibrium was steadily vanishing, and my leg had begun to swell from the fall. The endurance and coordination it took was a feat of Olympic proportions. Years later, like finding notes in an old, forgotten pocket, I was still happening upon the strangest items, with no memory of how or why I had chosen them or their location.

Upon our arrival at the hospital, I let the assumptions run their course—toxins in my body had accumulated from an untreated flu, developed into pneumonia, and I was just the victim of a random stroke of bad luck. I noted the date on the thick block of paper pinned to the wall. It was December 27th. I had been unconscious for two days. Since no one was suspicious in the emergency room, a toxicology screening was never conducted. My cover worked. Before the end of the day, I was admitted with a diagnosis of "dehydration resulting from pneumonia."

I don't recall the time I spent in ICU, but several days later I came to on the liver transplant floor, two days away from joining the list of people waiting for a donor. By fluke, a routine test had revealed a life-threatening level of proteins. Normal counts for a healthy liver measured somewhere around 50. Mine were at 18,000.

The queasiness that filled my body would have dwarfed even the most sadistic forms of medieval torture. I was desperately amenable to anything that would stop the nausea and profuse vomiting, even if it meant cutting an organ right out of my body. Fortunately within days, although still off the charts, my proteins count began to decline to safer ranges. Consequently, the twitching in my hands stopped and my speech returned to normal. Despite the dangers of keeping my secret, I had managed to survive.

Eight days after my admission, I was discharged to contend with the torment of my survival in the privacy of my own home. The physical aftermath continued with the commencement of passing hallucinations, and a private hell of insomnia began to run its course. Even if you were the most contented person alive, if the nausea didn't kill you, you would wish it had.

Waking Up

My free fall back into life had begun. It had begun with a masquerade, an inescapable momentum of falsehoods that I perpetuated every time I looked into the eyes of a loved one I had deceived. I had always prided myself on unwavering integrity. No one would have ever thought to question the honor of my word. However, in terms of the real truth, I had to answer to myself—and soon, even worse, to Dr. Joseph. Netted by fate, I had woken up.

CHAPTER 20

White Rage

January 2001

Scuba divers are instructed to follow the direction of their air bubbles if they ever become so disoriented that they can't figure out which way is up. I felt as though my oxygen tank had burst, and while I was frantically swimming upwards to the surface, I noticed that my air bubbles were going sideways.

The doctors had assured me of a full recovery and the nausea had dissipated, but I was still weeks away from being out of the woods. Combined with the residue of poisons still floating through my body, unrelenting physical suffering had only compounded my despair. I knew I couldn't go back to making another attempt. I knew I couldn't go forward to a future of misery. I knew I could not remain where I was. Hopelessness was a ravenous predator on the psychological food chain, and it was swallowing me whole. I realized that my only choice was to call Dr. Joseph. One week after my discharge from the hospital, I staggered into her office, commencing what would become a radical shift in the direction of our therapeutic journey.

I had always been habitually early for my appointments. Nervously, I waited outside her office door. She poked her head out, signaling me to come in with her customary, friendly wave. Our greetings never included physical touching. Thus, when she uncharacteristically reached over and tugged on the shoulder of my coat, as if to say, "Hey, it's so good to see you again!" I was stunned by the contact—a gesture that translated her sincere delight in our reunion. The distinctive sparkle of welcome in her eyes sent a torrent of guilt right through me. Dr. Joseph had trusted me, and I had broken my end of a very precious agreement. Why did she have to be so happy to see me? Resisting the temptation to turn around and retreat to my car, I took a seat and made my way through a minute or two of the usual, post-vacation inquiries.

"How are you feeling?" Cali eventually asked. Expecting to be kicked out the door within moments, I was puzzled by her sympathetic overtone.

"Not so good. I still have a long way to go before my liver heals," I replied.

"Liver? I thought it was your kidneys?"

"No, it's my liver." I had assumed all along that the inferences from liver damage would have raised enough suspicion for Cali to reach some fairly accurate conclusions about why I had been admitted to the hospital. However, her genuine concern instantly revealed that she had no idea what had really happened over Christmas. I was paralyzed by the fear and shame of confessing the details and instead, averted my eyes.

"Your sister-in-law called me to cancel the appointment we had scheduled for right after the holidays. She told me that you had pneumonia and kidney damage, but that you would be all right and would be in touch after you were discharged," she bewilderingly explained.

"Well, it must have been a misstatement because it was my liver. And, it's not what everyone thinks, anyway," I quietly began.

"I tried calling you in the hospital when I heard the news. They told me you were in ICU and not receiving calls. Didn't you get the messages I left with the nurses? I wanted to come see you," she continued. I could see that Dr. Joseph was terribly confused and that my words had not sunk in, yet.

"No, I didn't get any messages. I had the phone disconnected because I was too sick to speak to anyone. I didn't want any visitors, especially you. I couldn't face you," I hinted.

"Why not?" A hard, solemn expression immediately replaced the warmth of Dr. Joseph's smile.

"I assumed you knew," I stalled.

"Knew what?"

"I didn't keep my promises."

"What do you mean?" Cali's eyes squinted, wrinkled with a deepening frown.

"I O.D.'d," I confessed.

Silent tension filled the room and the air became almost too thick to breathe. Cali's heart appeared to have stopped and the racing of mine took up the extra beats.

"*What?*" Cali snapped.

"I overdosed." A long pause shifted the atmosphere to a frightening calmness. I could feel the cold sweat form on the back of my neck.

"What did you do?" she asked tersely, attempting to conceal what I later learned was a blinding, white rage.

"I tried to kill myself," I winced, eyes locked to the floor. My heart was pounding in my mouth, adrenaline pumping chaotically throughout my body.

"*What do you mean?* How?" Smoldering heat of fury radiated across the room.

"I really don't want to talk about it," I fearfully replied.

"Why not?"

"Because it's over and I don't want to go through the details."

"Well, I *want* to know the details," she demanded.

"Why?" I knew Cali was going to be insistent, but I resisted nonetheless. I was petrified that she would have me admitted to a psychiatric hospital—a consequence I feared if all agreements were off.

"Don't you think this was a significant event in your life?" Cali grimaced, as she queried.

"Yes," I answered. The therapeutic momentum gained speed.

"Do you think you are safe now?"

I hesitated for a moment, debating the consequences of my answer. Cali glared at me, waiting for the only undeniable response.

"Yeah, I guess," I whispered.

"You *guess*?"

"No. I know I am. For now anyway."

"Don't you think it's important for me to gather as many of the facts as I can?"

"Yeah," I reluctantly agreed. Each one of her questions was like an oral smelling salt, reviving me with logic.

"So, *what* did you do?"

"I took some pills, but somehow it didn't work and I woke up. A friend took me to the hospital." Despite my inability to gauge what was underlying Dr. Joseph's unsettling composure, I risked what I most feared, swallowed hard and continued to answer each question. It was clear, however, that this was a different side of Cali and there would be no more fucking around.

"Didn't they do a tox-screen in the emergency room?"

"No, I told them I had been fighting the flu. A doctor found a spot on my chest x-ray and somehow concluded it was pneumonia, so I went with it," I explained.

"Didn't they know you lost a spouse last year? Didn't they have a psychologist come speak to you? No one asked if you had tried to kill yourself?" Cali hammered away in utter disbelief.

"No. Well, they kept asking me if I took too much Tylenol—implying a suspicion, I suppose. But, no one asked. I really thought you knew," I said.

"If I had been told it was your liver, I may have suspected something. But, honestly Terry, I trusted you." Her words plunged through every moral principle I ever stood for.

"Do you want me not to come in anymore?" I braced myself, waiting for her to tell me that our trust had been irreparably destroyed and that she could no longer treat me.

"Do you really think you are worth that little?"

"Yeah," I murmured, awestruck by her response. I was sweltering in the fear of having divulged what I thought was one of the most destructive things I ever could have done to our relationship. Her words poured over me like an ice cold bucket of water, splashing me awake with new possibilities. Maybe she wasn't going to hospitalize me after all. My fear of being left to face my troubles without her began to ease as I started to understand her willingness to continue working with me. I would *never* forget the reassuring implication that I was still worth something to her.

"Do you really think I would terminate treatment? I've always told you, Terry, that there is *nothing* you could do that would make me kick you out of therapy. Nothing would make me give up on you."

"Well, I wouldn't blame you if you could no longer trust me," I said.

"There is no doubt that we have a lot of work to do, but I still trust you and I would never ask you to leave," she reiterated.

"I don't understand. To be brutally honest, don't you think that trusting me is a little foolish?" I was baffled. She didn't appear to be enraged, yet she wasn't exhibiting her usual disposition either.

"No, I don't think it's foolish. I have too much faith in you, Terry, and I won't let you die," Cali declared emphatically. "I can't explain it in words; it's just something that I feel. But, first we need to make sure you are safe in order to do this work. So, what do we do the next time you feel suicidal?" she asked.

"There won't be a next time."

"How do I know that?"

"I can't tell you. I would rather not answer than lie to you," I replied.

"You don't have that option anymore, Terry. You need to tell me what you're thinking." Cali's eyes were pushing me so hard that I felt as though my back was becoming part of the wall. I knew it would be self-defeating if I withheld what I was really feeling. If there was any chance I could be helped, she needed to know everything. I had gone this far with the truth and so I braved the answer.

"Because, I will never go through this again. And, even if I were to ever do so, it would not be an attempt. I would make sure that I died."

"What do you mean you would make sure?" I could see Cali hold her breath, clearly containing an outburst.

"I wouldn't take pills."

"What would you do?"

I squirmed in my seat, but Cali kept her eyes locked onto mine. "I would probably slit my wrists." Cali shuddered. "Well, you told me that you wanted me to be completely honest," I exclaimed.

"Yes, I did and thank you for telling me." I knew better than to be warmed by a traditional expression of gratitude. Her appreciation was merely a sanction of full disclosure. "I want to ask you something, but I can't until you first promise me that you are safe for now," she said.

"I am, Cali, I promise you."

Cali's glare reflected her deliberation and hesitance to continue. "What stopped you from cutting your wrists after you woke up?" she finally asked.

"You know that I couldn't deal with the mess," I joked.

"*Do you think that's funny?*" Cali retorted, her intolerance wiping the smirk right off my face.

"No," I said, instantly realizing that this was no time to try and lighten things up with anything comical. Cali let the silence force me to continue. "There are a bunch of reasons. Because, I thought it would be better if I looked like I was asleep and spared the people who would find me from the gore."

"That's very considerate of you, Terry," Cali replied. "What are the other reasons?"

I knew I shouldn't have prefaced that there was more than one reason, but there was no turning back. Cali would never have forgone the opportunity to force me to elucidate every thought in my head. "I didn't want to cut myself. It was hard enough to overcome my fears as it was," I said.

"What fears?"

"About the logistics."

"What are the logistics?"

"The preparation, deciding how to do it, how much to take, what to take—agonizing over all of the details. I was afraid it wouldn't work and that I would wake up—or worse, survive with brain damage," I said.

"You mean you were more concerned about the logistics than about the people in your life?" Cali seethed.

"No. I cared very much about the people I love."

"No, you didn't."

"Yes, I did, Cali. Just because I wanted to die doesn't mean that I didn't care about anyone else," I argued.

"Well, you may have cared, but you didn't care enough," she declared.

As fierce as this blow was, I could not refute its accuracy.

"Even if I wanted to, there's no way I could ever take anything again, anyway. My liver is in really bad shape, and the nausea has been horrendous. I can't even look at the stuff," I said.

"Where are the rest of the drugs now?"

"At home."

"So, what are we going to do?" she asked.

"I don't know, but I definitely won't take anything again." I already knew that handing over the key or making a promise would no longer suffice.

"Then give the drugs to me," she demanded.

"Fine," I quipped sarcastically, hoping it was a bluff. We were both equally surprised by my concession.

"Bring them in to me tomorrow morning. And, I want *all* of them, Terry—everything you have."

I knew better than to argue. My standard refusal would have been a clear indication that I did not really mean what I was saying, and I wanted to do anything that would help redeem myself. Unlike our past negotiations, I didn't dare ask for her promise to return my stash. Moreover, I was willing to agree to almost anything rather than let on that I was still hopeless. However, it was naive of me to believe that Cali wasn't keenly aware I was at rock bottom. In fact, that was the very reason she was pushing me so hard.

"I want you to promise me that you will not get any more drugs," she continued.

"O.K."

"No, Terry, I want to hear you promise me in a *full* sentence. I want you to look me in the eyes and tell me that you will not get any more drugs, that you will not drink or get high again."

"I can't drink, anyway. My liver is really bad, Cali."

"Fine. But, we know that once you feel better, things will change, and you will forget how it felt. I want you to promise me," she insisted.

There was no denying that in the past, I had falsely assured myself I was done with abusing drugs and alcohol. After visibly struggling in silence, I pulled my eyes from the floor. "I promise," I muttered.

"No, I want to hear you say it in a full sentence. I want to make sure we aren't missing anything, that there aren't any omissions or misunderstandings," she persisted.

I took a deep breath. "I promise that I won't get any more drugs and that I won't drink or get high."

"There is no more bullshitting, Terry. This is it. Either you make a commitment to this process or you don't. I can't do the work with you if I have to worry about your getting so upset or pissed off that you terminate therapy. Walking out will be a scenario that is re-enacted over and over again, and I'm not going to take that chance. I will do whatever I need to do to save your life, and I will remain as available to you as I can, but there are going to be conditions."

"O.K., I promise," I said, attempting to pre-empt her. I knew exactly what was coming next.

"I want you to look at me and say the words."

"I promise I won't leave therapy," I stuttered. I don't know who was more exasperated at this point, but I was getting my first peek at Cali's simmering rage. I knew she both wanted to help me and strangle me at the same time. "I won't leave, but I don't know how I'm going to keep adjusting to the loneliness and being apart from you in between appointments. The separations are just too painful for me."

"I understand that it's difficult for you to deal with the limitations that are inherent to our relationship, but as I've always promised you, we can work anything out, *anything*, as long as we continue to talk. I guess what you have to decide is whether or not being in therapy is worth tolerating some of those painful feelings for now," Cali said.

Often, the most significant turning points during the therapeutic process occurred with the simplest, peripheral statements. I had no idea how I was going to continue struggling with our time apart, but Cali was right. If I was going to live, something of her was better than nothing of her. It was this very point that sealed my decision to endure the conflict and remain in therapy.

I was so tired and overwhelmed that I couldn't think straight. Promises to relinquish the drugs, stay straight and commit to treatment were a good start. But, depression was self-perpetuating. The very existence of it was preventing me from making the decisions that were necessary to eradicate it, and my downward spiral continued. As I sat in silence, Cali sensed my desperation, and somehow, knew that it was time for her to take charge.

"Terry, I know how you feel about it, but it's time for you to trust my years of experience. *You are going to take anti-depressants.* Either you call your doctor, or I'm giving you the number of a psychiatrist. Which one is it going to be?"

This was the first time Cali explicitly ordered me to do anything. Typically, she advocated that the power of making my own decisions would force me to take responsibility for myself, but Christmas day had thrust us into new territory where many of the traditional rules no longer applied. I was too weak, too vulnerable, too everything to battle it out and, ambivalently, I took refuge in her guidance.

"I'll take the number from you," I quietly agreed. Cali handed me a slip of paper with the name and number of Dr. Rebecca Berman.

"Terry, this is the best decision you've made in months. Anti-depressants won't be a panacea; they are a tool to help you feel better while we do the work. Dr. Berman is an expert and you can trust her." The muscles in Cali's face began to relax. She had finally loosened the foothold on months of my defiant refusals to take any medication.

"I just don't want to feel artificial."

"I promise you, Terry, you won't feel artificial. There are many different medications to choose from until we find what's right for you," Cali explained. "I want you to call Dr. Berman as soon as you leave here, and *be aggressive* about contacting her, Terry. I will call you in one hour to see when you've scheduled the appointment."

Suddenly, I realized that I hadn't thought about the time. I glanced over at the clock to find that we had been talking for over an hour. Dr. Joseph had not allowed the constraints of time to interfere with what would become some of the most important work we had ever done. Surprisingly relieved, I left her office feeling the most protected from myself than I had been in years.

CHAPTER 21

Everything Left to Lose

February 2001

Finding empathy for a suicide attempt is as unlikely as killing your parents and receiving sympathy because you are an orphan. An essential predicate to my emotional health was to reduce my isolation. Ironically, that very sense of alienation was perpetuated by having to live in a private world of suicidal thoughts that I could not share with anyone—or so I thought.

It would take up to a few weeks for the medication prescribed by Dr. Berman to reach a dose of therapeutic value. Still mystified by their fortitude, I felt my organs begin to slowly recuperate. In the interim, boredom and loneliness had become cohabitating squatters, and I bore the challenge of occupying my mind. I was too weak and nauseous to eat, exercise, or interact with people. My days of emptiness were of an excruciating duration.

Over the next several appointments, Dr. Joseph's approach became a delicate balance between despotic and compassionate—mindful of my vulnerabilities and sorrow, yet diligent in her quest to reach me. If anything was to be gained from Christmas, it was the blaring message that there was no more time to dance around and I could no longer wrap my past in refusals based on irrelevance.

"Did you tell anyone that you were thinking of killing yourself?" Dr. Joseph asked.

"No, of course not. I would never have wanted anyone to feel guilty that they should have done something to prevent it," I retorted.

"Who are you closest to right now?" Cali asked.

In the moments before answering, a litany of names ran through my mind. Sadly, I noted how short the list had become through the years of distancing myself from the people who cared about me.

"Probably my cousin Clarence. And, Paul and Rose. They are like family to me."

"Don't you think they would have felt guilty, anyway— because you *didn't* talk to them about how you were feeling beforehand?" Cali asked.

"Definitely not," I replied, confident in the absurdity of her suggestion.

"Terry, how would you feel if one of them killed themselves and you had no idea how they felt? If you were that close, close enough to feel like family, wouldn't you have held yourself responsible for not picking up on things?"

"No," I answered, although I could already feel Cali's words hammering a crack in my conviction.

"In fact, maybe it would have caused them even *more* guilt because, knowing you as they do, they missed the signs that could have been right before their eyes. If there was anything they wouldn't forgive themselves for, it would be that, don't you think?"

"So, what should I have done? Tell them that I was going to kill myself?" I asked, struggling to hold onto my more forgivable perspective. Consistent with her usual practice, Cali did not answer my question, and instead turned the focus back onto what I thought.

"Wouldn't *you* have wanted them to talk to you first?" she asked.

"Yes, I would have wanted the chance to comfort them and hopefully, be there to help talk them through the pain. But, it's different with me," I replied. The last thing I wanted to learn was that the importance of being an honest, sincere friend included a moral obligation to tell others about my plans.

"I see. You're the exception," Cali said, with a sarcastic nod of her head.

"I don't mean to sound like a hypocrite. It's just that, unlike most people, I wasn't doing it for attention or as a call for help—I didn't want anyone to prevent me from doing it," I explained.

"What do you think would have happened after they heard you were dead?" Cali asked.

"I don't know—they would be upset. But, they'd go on— they have spouses, children, jobs, and other things that fill their lives."

"Hmmm, well let's talk about that. What would have happened to your best friend Paul?" Cali dug in.

"I don't know."

"'I don't know' is not good enough, Terry. What would have happened to him?"

"Once when I was sick, he told me that if I died, he would be all alone. I knew it was overstated, but I also knew exactly what he meant. We've been best friends forever. We were next-door neighbors growing up, and practically lived at each other's houses. There isn't anyone else who would understand our families, or the dynamics of each of our upbringings like the two of us would for each other. I know I would be a huge loss to him, but he has a wife, children, and a thriving business. His life would go on," I argued.

"Do you really think any of those things would compensate him for losing you? How would *you* feel if *he* died? Would your job, or any other part of your life for that matter, fill that hole?"

"No," I had to admit.

"Would anyone ever be able to replace him?"

"No."

"Wouldn't the pain impact *you* for the rest of *your* life?"

"Yes."

"How do you think it would have affected your niece?"

"I don't know," I answered, trying to pry away from her determination.

"Not good enough."

"She wouldn't know her aunt," I answered.

"You've told me how much your niece looks up to you. She's 10 years old and she *would* remember. What do you think the adults in your family would tell her?"

"I don't know." Prompted to resume from the tenacity in Cali's eyes, I continued, answering as evasively as possible. "They would tell her that I died."

"Let's play it out. Would they lie to her, or would they tell her the truth? What, specifically, would they say to her?"

"They probably would have to be truthful and tell her that I killed myself." My eyes dropped to the floor. I hated having to say the words that brought the horrid consequences to life. But, that was the very strategy behind Dr. Joseph's approach.

"What kind of example do you think you would set for her? How would she be affected?"

"Well, obviously, she would be pained at first. But, I think if they explained how I was feeling, eventually she would understand."

"Is that *really* what you believe?" Cali immediately called me on my nonsense.

"No," I confessed. Another therapeutic moment was realized as I was forced to *feel*, rather than intellectualize, the impact my suicide would have had on the rest of my niece's life.

"Paul probably would have been the one who found your body. Do you think *that* would have had a distinct effect on him?"

"Yes," I shamefully answered.

"What would have happened to your cousin, Clarence?"

"Same answer," I replied, desperately wishing to put an end to her line of questioning. I sensed now that her words were no longer really questions, but statements that were blasting my resolve to bits.

"What would have happened to Clarence? Would you have left a hole in his life that only you could have filled?"

"Yes. But, we don't need to go through each and every family member. I know what the fallout would have been."

"*You do?* Well then, tell me. What would the fallout have been like *for me*? What would have happened to me?

"We really don't need to talk about this, Cali."

"Why not?" she asked, overcoming my attempted refusal to answer with her habitual, back-door approach: Answer the question or explain why I was *not* answering the question. Either way, what she asked was going to be discussed.

"Because, I already know the personal consequences to others."

"So, if you already know, then it should be easy to tell me."

I paused, squirming in my seat, reeled in by the hook I had just swallowed.

"You would probably feel responsible and take a leave of absence from work. Someone in my family might sue you. You would start second-guessing your decisions and, as you've told me, would have a hole in your heart. But, you would travel, raise your children, and eventually resume your life. Cali, I really don't think we need to talk about this anymore." I could hardly stand the vivid thoughts of suffering that Cali's questions painted for me.

"Is this hard for you to think about?" she asked, intent on provoking that very response.

"Yes," I answered.

"Why? Because you don't want to have to *really* think about the consequences?"

"Partly. I just don't want to cause anyone pain," I said contritely.

"But, you *almost did* cause tremendous pain for a lot of people. I don't think you have a clue how your death would have affected them, or me. You said 'partly.' What's the other part?" Cali replied, tenaciously dissecting every syllable of my answer.

"I just don't want any of it to matter," I sighed.

"What's 'it'?"

"You, people, everything. I mean, why do I have to live like this? Don't you think there are circumstances where people who are suffering should be able to end their own lives?"

"Yes. I think what your husband did was understandable. But, you are not terminally ill, and you can get better."

As though freshly struck by the notion that Kurt chose to end his life, Cali's statement took my breath away. No one had ever actually voiced the words that described the circumstances that precipitated Kurt's death. Unexpectedly, I began to fight back tears as the heartache I thought I had long since put to rest began to linger again.

"But, if I'm this miserable, then I'm just living for other people. In a way, aren't they being selfish? Because, if you really cared about me, you wouldn't want me to live like this," I argued. I could feel Kurt hovering over me, wringing his hands.

"I definitely don't want you to live like this. But, if you were physically sick and the doctor said that in order to save your life, you would have to endure a painful shot, I would insist on the shot. Your situation is not like Kurt's. You don't have to die from depression and, although the process can sometimes be agonizing, there are things we can do to help you feel more comfortable and feel the joys of being alive," Cali replied.

"You don't understand. I can't be more comfortable. As soon as I begin to care about anything, the bottom just drops out from under me. Or, whatever I care about inevitably ends up causing me pain. Sometimes, there are things that just *aren't* resolvable," I said.

"Like what?" she asked.

"Like the rules that limit our contact. After I leave here today, I will have to deal with the pain of adjusting to your absence, of feeling like an outsider, all over again. I just wish I had the freedom not to care anymore than I already do," I sadly replied.

"But, Terry, sometimes you have to feel the bad in order to feel the good. You can't be selective about some feelings without cutting off all the others," Cali began to explain.

"Why not? If I can make what is hurting me not matter as much, then wouldn't I be better off?"

"No, because then you will be dead inside. If you numb yourself from pain or the discomfort of difficult feelings, you will also prevent yourself from feeling joy. You can't choose to have one feeling, but then not another. It just doesn't work that way," Cali continued.

"I don't understand why not," I argued.

"Well, for example, do you feel safe and cared about when you come here?"

"Yes."

"Does that feel good to you?"

"Yes."

"And, do you care about me?"

"Yes."

"Do you think, if you made me matter less, that those feelings of safety and being cared about would remain unaffected?"

"I don't know."

"Well, this relationship *does* matter to you, right?"

"Yes." At first, I couldn't help but notice Dr. Joseph's liberal use of the term "relationship," which I typically associated with spouses, or significant others. However, over time I learned her strategy was based on a more literal usage: As I became attuned to her repeated use of the term, I subconsciously accepted that I had a connection to her, to *someone*. She used us as a starting point for me to re-connect and form many different levels of relationships with others.

"Then, what do you think you would lose if you made me or this process not matter?"

"I don't know," I answered.

"Not good enough, Terry."

"I don't know if it would be considered a loss because, if you didn't matter, then I wouldn't struggle with the time apart in between sessions."

"But, if I don't matter to you, then how can you hold onto the good feelings you get from this relationship—the very feelings that have made me matter to you?"

"I don't know," I stubbornly answered, already feeling my understanding shift as I inched away from my quest to shut down.

"Do you *really* want to make us not matter? Because, if you do, then you will ensure the loss of the good feelings as well. Do you understand?"

"Yeah, mostly," I replied.

"I don't want you to feel discomfort from our relationship, and I believe, 100 percent, that we can work anything out so that you don't have to keep suffering. But, you have to keep talking to me until we understand it better. Tell me what you need, what you want, so that I have the chance to give it to you, or if I can't, then *we* have the chance to find a compromise until we both feel more comfortable. I want to show you how to use our relationship to practice this, so that you can have more fulfilling relationships in your life."

My brain pulsated with the exhaustion of being stretched in so many new directions, and I was almost certain that Cali wasn't far behind me. The session had been tedious, but the intensity was necessary in order to shake the roots of many of my long-standing beliefs. This was the first time I felt my rationalization that no one would be seriously affected by my suicide being jeopardized. Further, I was forced to re-evaluate the misconception that my silence would have spared people a lifetime of guilt and reluctantly, began to entertain the notion that I was actually hurting them more by NOT telling them what I was feeling.

Whether or not I fully understood or agreed with Dr. Joseph didn't even matter at that point in time. The seeds of her questions were already bursting through the soil of my world. Despite remaining torn about the therapeutic limitations, I was already unwilling to sacrifice the feelings between us. And, as I stood up to leave her office, the meaning of a favorite Janice Joplin lyric that I had glossed over for years, began to play a new and more literal hum through my mind:

"Freedom is just another word for nothing left to lose."

CHAPTER 22

The Plant

March 2001

Ejected from death's canon, the fingers of mortality had plucked me out of the tumble and flung me back into the chair at Dr. Joseph's office. Although I was still whirling in despair, my mind had clearly begun to increase its attendance. Fortunately, not only did I respond to the anti-depressant medication, but I was so ultra-sensitive that it only took days, rather than the norm of weeks, before I began to feel its subtle effects. It wasn't long before my years of stubborn resistance were eclipsed by the realization that I had suffered unnecessarily for so long.

For the very first time, I made a commitment to therapy without the company of a plan for my death. Embarking on this journey was much like adapting to life after severing my Siamese twin. I now had to feel and think about everything that I had not wanted to matter. With death as the ante, life had forced my hand, laying down its royal flush when I didn't even have a pair. Apparently, I didn't yet know the rules. It was time for me to learn.

"Terry, I've been wondering about something," Cali began. "E-mailing a patient in between sessions is new for me. And, it led me to think about what you would do if I said something that left you feeling unsettled."

"Well, I would try to accept it and deal with it," I shrugged.

"Would that be possible?" she asked.

"No, I suppose not," I replied, not really supposing.

"What effect do you think your not speaking up would have?"

"I don't know."

"Well, take a guess. I won't hold you to it."

"It would probably continue to gnaw at me, and my first impulse would be to withdraw to protect myself—even though I know that protecting myself would be impossible," I admitted.

"I would never want you to accept anything that bothers you. I would always want you to keep coming after me, and to keep telling me what you need. And, if you were still not satisfied with my response, don't give up until you get what you want, or we figure out a compromise. You don't have to live with the intolerable. Don't back off, Terry."

"I don't have much choice, anyway," I said.

"What do you mean?" Cali asked.

"Well, it looks like life called my bluff. I would *have to* think about all of those things now."

"I don't understand," Cali replied.

"It's not literally a bluff. What I mean is that now I have to face things. I know this sounds strange, but there is a certain amount of emotional freedom when you intend to kill yourself," I began, surprising myself with the concept.

"I'm not sure if I understand what you're saying. Tell me again," Cali implored.

"Because I was going to die, I did not have to deal with my future. I didn't have to worry about getting sick, or how I was going to pay my bills, or fear losing someone I love. Of course, I thought about all of these things before, and they were a big part of what led up to Christmas. But, in a way, planning my death was an escape that protected me from life," I explained.

"And, in a way, it also *prevented* you from living your life," Cali emphatically corrected. "So, are you now trying to figure out how to live, instead of die?" she asked, unable to hide the glee in her eyes.

"Yeah, I guess so."

I could see Cali's face light up with the affirmation.

"Have you taken down your sign yet?" Cali teased, referencing her flippant suggestion months before that I should place a sign on my doorway with the motto, 'I don't want it to matter.'

"Let's not get too hasty," I answered with a smirk, relieved that the climate had shifted to the lighter mood neither of us had felt in months, if ever. The look in Cali's eyes revealed the shared sentiment.

"But, now it feels like my thoughts about suicide have only been replaced with another set of worries."

"What worries are you not telling me about?" she asked, getting down to the business of living.

"The future," I sarcastically answered, unable to resist countering her question with a vague response.

"Can you try to narrow it down?"

"I'm worried that I will have to live my life being this unhappy," I revealed.

"Well, sometimes, it's difficult to begin feeling better."

"Why?"

"Because often people resist feeling things that are unfamiliar to them," Cali began to explain.

"That's ridiculous. I would definitely let myself feel happier, if I could. I wouldn't resist it—I'd be relieved."

"I know that you *want* to feel better, but you underestimate the capacity of your mind to fool you. Sometimes people unconsciously hold onto emotions. They say they don't care, because they care too much. Or, they deny certain feelings like anger, sadness or hope because it's more familiar and safer," Cali explained.

"Feeling unhappy does not feel safer to me. It's not like I choose to feel this way, like I'm voluntarily holding onto a choice from a menu. Why wouldn't I admit to wanting to feel better?"

"Because your history has taught you to be on guard for the next disaster, and even bet on its occurrence, and to protect yourself from it. There is a wall we keep smacking up against, Terry, but just like you, everyone in the universe has some resistance to the unknown. This is why I continually tell you to talk and talk. Because knowing your fears is how change begins."

"Cali, I fully resist the notion that I am resisting anything. Maybe the reason it's so hard to feel happier is because there's nothing that will be able to help me feel better about life, including this process. Maybe my view of myself and the world *can't* be changed," I retorted.

"But your worldview isn't working, Terry. We can't change the past, but we can certainly impact the future. *History is not destiny.* You don't have to give into thinking that your sadness is an inevitability," Cali urged. "What would it mean for you to feel happier, to stop all the crummy things you feel? What feelings would fill your life?"

"Well, obviously I would fill my life with things that made me happier," I answered, exasperated. "If I wasn't looking to do that, why would I keep coming here?"

"Walking into this office doesn't preclude your resistance to things that are too scary for you to face," Cali explained.

"Like what?"

"Like, why can't you even own a plant?"

"That was a long time ago," I answered, stunned that she remembered.

Months earlier, I briefly mentioned refusing a plant as a gift from a friend. Even the question caused me to feel suffocated by the thought of taking responsibility for a life—any life, including a plant.

"Do you have any plants in your house now?" she asked.

"No. Just because I don't ever want to take care of anything again doesn't mean I'm afraid of feeling better. The two are not related," I stubbornly replied.

"So, the fact that you won't allow another living thing to reside in your house is random and has no relationship to anything that has happened to you?"

"No. Well, obviously it's related to feeling exhausted from the way I spent my life over the past four or five years. But, it's not because I'm afraid. I need a break, and I just don't want to be responsible for feeding or taking care of another thing."

"Are you saying that you aren't afraid to care about anything?"

"No," I had to admit. Our recent discussions about my fear of being exposed or vulnerable were fresh in both of our minds.

"Terry, that's what I am talking about. Maybe your resistance is due to a fear, the fear of taking the risk of caring again," she explained.

"Awhhh," I moaned, slowly shaking my head. "It sounds so damn textbook."

"Textbook or not, I believe it's accurate. Do you agree?"

"Maybe," I sighed. "But I don't think you really understand what things were like for me when Kurt was sick."

"Maybe I don't. So, tell me," Cali persisted.

"I wouldn't even know where to begin. It's too overwhelming."

"So, pick any place. Things don't have to be organized before you speak," she reminded me.

"But it would be impossible for you to understand unless you knew everything. That's the problem, because the effect on me wasn't just the result of one thing or one event. It was the culmination of everything," I explained.

"That's okay, Terry. We will keep talking until I understand everything. I really want to know what it was like for you. Just start anywhere."

"It's very hard for me. I realize it was a horrible situation, but it feels like I'm pitying myself too much when I try to talk about it," I said.

"What's wrong with a little self-pity?" she asked.

"Because feeling sorry for myself is unappreciative of what I do have."

"What do you mean?"

"I'm healthy, in my 30s, and I have an education. It's not like I live on the street with no income and three mouths to feed," I explained.

"Terry, you took care of your husband, who you loved so much, for four years, and then he died and left you a 35 year-old widow. Do you think acknowledging how terrible that is makes you unappreciative?"

"No."

"If the roles were reversed, and you were talking to your best friend, wouldn't you agree that she had every reason to be upset about what she had endured?"

"Perhaps," I answered, feeling my opinion begin to spin in a new direction.

"There is nothing wrong with feeling sorry for yourself. It's not an either-or situation. You can still be appreciative of everything you have at the same time you mourn all you've lost," Cali pointed out.

"I think I'm still shell-shocked by a lot of it. It's strange because I lived with the illness for so long. But, sometimes it feels like it wasn't me—like it was another life altogether. Then again, other times it feels like it was the only life I've ever had, completely consuming me."

"Again, it's not either-or. *Both* emotions can co-exist," she replied. "I'm sorry that we have to end now," Cali said, alerting me to the time. "But I want to understand more about how your life was with Kurt. Will you tell me more about it the next time I see you?" she asked.

"Yeah, I suppose," I replied, with mixed feelings about ever continuing the discussion.

"Hold down the enthusiasm, Terry, it's overwhelming me," she joked. "I'll see you next time."

"So, how are you feeling about what we discussed during our last appointment?" Cali began before I even took a seat.

"Whoa. Don't hold back on account of me, Cali," I replied.

"Do you want to talk about other things before we get back to how it felt for you when Kurt was sick?" Cali insinuated the inevitability of our discussion.

"I guess not."

"So, what do you think the hardest part of your life was while Kurt had ALS?" Cali asked, putting an end to my sarcasm.

"The paralysis of his tongue—no question. The consequences were infinite. You would think that the worst part was his speech impairment. But, that didn't even compare to the dozens of other unseen ramifications," I explained.

"Like what?" Cali asked.

"Mostly, it was the effect it had on our emotional intimacy. Like losing the ability to kiss, for example. Imagine making love without *ever*, not even once, kissing. Imagine not being able to greet each other, or comfort, or thank one another with the softness of that kind of touch. It's something that is unique to the two of you, and when you lose it, you lose a very important form of expression." The memory was gutwrenching and I could feel myself starting to well up inside.

"That sounds really tough," Cali acknowledged.

"You see, most people were only able to see the surface of things. But, for me, the most obvious losses didn't even rival the obscure, insidious nuances of every *single* symptom," I said, exasperated with the resurgence of memories.

"Tell me more."

"The tone of his voice was another monstrosity. No matter how tired or frustrated I felt, I had to develop a superhuman amount of patience."

"Why? What do you mean?"

"Kurt began to sound like a cross between the Cookie Monster and a very baritone Oscar the Grouch. I'm not kidding," I described.

"No, what do you mean by superhuman patience?" Cali asked.

"The noise coming at me was a distorted reality, and adapting to his tone required me to completely rewire my reflexes. Regardless of his mood, Kurt *always* sounded angry. You know because of the home I grew up in, I am ultra, ultra-sensitive to disrespect, particularly between spouses. I would *never* put up with that kind of shit from him, or anyone else under other circumstances."

"Couldn't you figure out his mood?" asked Cali.

"Not all the time. Because his face was paralyzed, he couldn't even disarm his words with a compassionate expression. So, I had to alter my instincts, and continually remind myself not to react defensively."

"What was the emotional cost for you?" Cali asked.

"It was a horrible situation for both of us. I felt so bad for him. But again, for me, it was another interference with being intimate. How would you feel if your husband always sounded like a drill sergeant, no matter what he was saying? Would the words 'I love you' feel the same without a tender voice?" I asked, imploring her to understand.

"Could anyone else understand his speech?" she asked.

"Yes, in the beginning. Actually, he never lost his ability to make sounds. But, it was as though he spoke a language that only the two of us mastered fluently. As time went on, fewer and fewer people were able to decipher his words, and I became his full-time interpreter. You can't imagine the personal consequences that resulted from *that*," I explained.

"You are right. I can't imagine, Terry. But, I want to understand, and I want you to tell me how it felt, how you are feeling now as you remember and talk about it."

"It's a mix of emotions. It's a combination of anger, sadness and anxiety. I know it's important for you to understand what it was like, but it's just too much to think about all at once."

"So, let's try not to think about it all at once. Again, why don't you try to just take things one at a time?" Cali suggested. "What comes to mind?"

"The incredible power of the tongue. You wouldn't believe what losing the mobility of that one organ impacts," I began, feeling myself well up again.

"How does talking about this make you feel?" Cali asked, noticing the change in my eyes.

"Exhausted just thinking about it, and lonely, too," I replied, flooded with the memories.

"Why does talking about it make you feel lonely?"

"It's not really because of the talking. It's because I'm reminded of how impossible it was for anyone to truly understand the magnitude of what we *both* had to endure," I answered.

"Let's just focus on you right now. What were the other consequences you felt?" Cali askcd.

"I had to become Kurt's full-time interpreter. Even when he was still understandable, I had to step in. Whenever he became slightly emotional, the ALS made the muscles and nerves in his face uncontrollable, preventing him from being able to speak," I explained.

"What would happen when you stepped in?"

"A lot of things. Kurt completely lost his autonomy, and I felt like an intruder. I didn't want to be part of his conversations, but I had to be present to help him communicate with everyone. I was a part of his every syllable, even when it was a disagreement. Under normal circumstances, it would have been enormously uncomfortable for me to be privy to those conversations. I was not only forced to be present, but I also had to become a participant," I said.

"And, how are you feeling now?" Cali asked.

"Terribly guilty," I said, loathing the memory.

"Why do you feel guilty?"

"Because, my troubles paled in comparison. Kurt was the one struggling to speak and face a terminal illness, not me," I said.

"Terry, I'm sure it was horrible. But, in many ways you were also condemned. Because it was *his* illness doesn't mean you didn't suffer along side of him," Cali suggested.

"It's not just guilt either. I'm frustrated and really pissed off," I continued, starting to feel the days coming back to life.

"Why?"

"Because, the inequities were outrageous. Being his personal interpreter was very different from being a professional interpreter, where the role is more of a removed bystander. The perception was that Kurt's words were my own, as though I was the one making the statements. Even though I spoke immediately following his garbled sounds, the words were coming out of *my* mouth. It was often impossible for anyone to remain aware that I was only the conduit of sound, and sometimes, it even appeared as though I was in agreement with whatever he was saying, even when I wasn't."

"How did you manage it?" Cali asked.

"I trained myself to un-feel the sounds coming from my lips, as though they were being played through a tape recorder. Except, I *wasn't* a tape recorder. Any of my personal feelings had to be quashed, even when I so disagreed with the content," I explained. The thought of what I had to do began choking the breath right out of me all over again.

"Why couldn't he just write or type what he wanted to say?"

"Because the nerve degeneration in his hands and fingers confiscated that personal liberty, too. By the time he died, his entire body had become almost completely paralyzed. We got some communication equipment, so he could use the computer keyboard by moving his head, but that was painstakingly slow, and typically, much more cumbersome than just making a go of it verbally."

"Sounds exhausting."

"We couldn't have a *healthy* argument like normal spouses. He couldn't call me to say hello anymore, or joke with me and make me laugh like he used to," I explained. My heart ached for the humor that had been the treasured core of our relationship.

"You must feel very sad thinking about this," Cali surmised.

"Well, I know it sounds strange to say, but it actually pisses me off."

"Why?"

"Because I never even got to be in denial about his illness. I couldn't avoid *talking* about ALS, because I had to do all of the speaking, including the ongoing explanations of his condition. And, because I was interpreting, I had to *listen* to the tone of his voice, a constant reminder that he was dying right before my eyes."

"I don't think that's strange at all. In fact, it makes a lot of sense that you would feel angry. Who wouldn't want to be in denial under those circumstances? By silently shouldering the bulk of those responsibilities, you gave others the luxury of something you could not afford."

Thinking back, I realized that, much like the Pied Piper, everyone had followed Kurt's lead while I, instead, honed my ability to internalize my suffering, as my words became less of my own.

"Didn't you talk to anyone about how you were feeling?" Cali continued.

"No, not really. I didn't want to sound like I was the victim. I just never dreamed of how far-reaching the consequences would be." The memories were overwhelming. The more I spoke to Cali, the more I realized that my deadened reflexes had begun to come alive, but the blindness of my senses were still adapting to the arrival of sight.

"I understand that Kurt was suffering from a horrible disease. That is a given, and we both know that you always remained sensitive to that. But don't you think you were a victim of ALS, too?" Cali asked.

"I'm wiped out, Cali. I don't think I have much more in me to continue talking about this," I sighed, wanting to get off the subject of martyrdom immediately.

"Alright. We can talk about it next time. But we will talk more about it," Cali declared.

"I don't doubt it for a moment," I said, as I stood up to leave.

Not thinking about it was no longer an option.

CHAPTER 23

Attention

March 2001

Although I had become much more amenable to the interrelationship between past and present, finding historically credible explanations for my feelings was not the easiest of tasks for Dr. Joseph. Our work continued forward like psychological archeology, as if the roots of my every emotion were being unearthed and dusted off with her feather brush. With the expectant vacillations, our journey continued as the therapeutic process evolved into an inextricable mix of e-mails and sessions.

"Why are you so opposed to acknowledging you may have been a victim?" Cali said, wasting no time getting to the point.

"Because I don't want to moan about it, or play the martyr. I really regret how much I said about myself last session," I answered.

"Why do you regret that? Aren't we here for you? I want to know how *you* feel regardless of the image you think it portrays," Cali reminded me once again. "Why do you deny yourself the right to feel badly about what was happening to you?"

"Because, I never want to look like I was taking care of Kurt to get attention from others."

"Why not? What's wrong with receiving attention?"

"Because, it's just wrong," I replied, feeling my face becoming red hot.

"What are you anxious about?" Cali asked, noticing the change in color.

"I don't know."

"Well, take a guess."

"I really don't know," I honestly repeated.

"Try to figure it out, Terry. Just use any words you can find," Cali pushed.

"It makes me feel like my family, and I *never* want to be like them," I said hesitantly, terrified of suggesting the idea of unbalanced genetics.

"What do you mean?" Cali asked, eager to seize the opportunity to hear more about my childhood.

"Remember that I told you when I was younger, I was very shy and introverted? Well, I grew up in a household where emotions were volatile and extreme. There were members of my family who thrived on despair, desperately using drama to get attention. I'm not exaggerating when I say this—there was always a perpetual crisis," I emphasized. My face cooled, as I felt my anxiety transform into the all-too-familiar childhood tension I had so detested.

"What did you feel like as that quiet child?" Cali asked.

"Stuck. There wasn't much emphasis placed on maintaining confidences, and I was often embarrassed by the exposure of my personal life. I remember recoiling from the exaggerated melodrama. You know how private I am. I'd rather be more honest with my emotions," I said.

"Why do you feel that expressing your emotions is anything but honest?" she asked.

"Because, I feel dishonest if it's to seek attention, and I've always avoided it at all costs," I explained.

"But, aren't there times when getting attention is appropriate?"

"Yeah, I suppose," I replied, wondering where Cali was going.

"In many ways, it seems that you've been living on the flip side of the same coin. You say that people in your family sought excessive amounts of attention, while you rejected anything that felt like it. Your way appears to be the opposite, but it is equally as extreme. Obviously, you have to see the connection between your upbringing and the way you avoid attention."

"Cali, I'm not going to cop out with the 'It-was-all-my-parents'-fault-syndrome,'" I answered.

"I'm not looking to blame your parents, or anyone else, for how you feel. There is a big difference between blame and finding the causes, or the contributing factors, that led to how you feel today. What if some of the things you feel *are* a result of the environment you were brought up in?" Cali asked.

"I won't sit here and say, 'Poor me, I was so neglected or abused', or blame anyone else for the way that I feel. Even if I agreed with the connection, it doesn't matter. I still take full responsibility for how I conduct my life now," I insisted.

"But, what do you think it cost you to deny yourself any attention?"

"Being too quiet, I suppose," I answered.

"What else?" Cali prodded.

"I don't know," I said, unwilling to proceed in the direction that I was somehow victimized.

"Do you think that by fanatically striving to be the *anti-family*, you prevented yourself from ever having a choice about what to feel?"

"What do you mean? I don't understand," I replied, perplexed.

"You have been so busy automatically rejecting *anything and everything* that felt like your family, that you haven't given yourself the freedom to choose who and what *you* want to *be*. Do you understand what I'm saying?"

"Not really," I answered.

"Let me try to put it another way that is clearer. Maybe there were qualities about them that you *would* have chosen to feel, and it *would've* been okay for you to be like them in those respects. And maybe there were other things that you would *not* have chosen to feel, because there were ways in which you did *not* want to be like them. But, by rejecting *everything*, you didn't even give yourself the choice of what you wanted to accept or reject," Cali explained.

"Well, it's a stretch, but I understand your point," I responded.

"Will you just give some thought to the possibility that, because of this, you've denied yourself the attention that you may have needed to feel better?"

"Okay, I'll try to think about it, Cali," I replied, feeling a stirring inside as I began to entertain an altogether different perception of the ingredients of my life.

1:27 P.M.

Cali,

Well, I guess it didn't take long for me to begin processing what we talked about today. It's an absolute miracle I didn't have a car accident on my way home from your office, and I couldn't wait to get home so I could write to you about what I think I've figured out.

Do you remember the confrontation that occurred between Kurt's business partner, George, and me a couple of years ago? You and I talked about it during the time I came in for treatment while Kurt was still alive. I had left my job to work with Kurt so he could sustain his business. Not long afterwards, Kurt and George began to have disagreements over their partnership, and George tried to take control of the business.

Well, I started thinking about my reaction to George's accusations, when he told me that I was the one who was responsible for turning Kurt against him and destroying their relationship. At the time, I disagreed with your belief that the extremity of my anger, while justifiable, was disproportionate, and that there had to be something more historical underlying my rage. I never understood or agreed with that proposition until just now.

I realize what my gnawing feelings were about. It was the fear that I was enjoying the attention I was getting from taking care of Kurt and something as horrific as ALS. I loved him and wanted to do so, but there was also a perception that I was an exceptional person for making those sacrifices. By not acknowledging the good I was doing, George did NOT give me that attention. But, deep inside, I was torn. I didn't want to admit that the attention was making me feel good, and that NOT getting it from George was upsetting me. I think I hated him even more for making me feel the conflict and self-loathing. It all makes so much more sense to me now.

I also realize that this cycle has affected so many other aspects of my life. For example, how I feel about my appearance. I don't want to say that I look good because it's vain and seeks attention. But, I don't want to say that I don't look good because I will then be getting attention for being modest. Or, I will be seeking attention for having a poor self-image because I was "abused" as a child. The turmoil continues because I honestly don't like the way I look. So, I don't want to discuss how I feel, but then, I don't want to discuss not discussing it, and blah, blah, blah.

The conflict continues when I space out in your office, or when my legs move—indicating that I'm anxious. I worry I've done these things to draw your attention. But maybe it's not contrived and would just happen anyway, or, I don't even fucking know anymore. But then I think I do know, because I feel all this guilt about it. It feels so dishonest. And now I think that I must have fooled you into caring about me, and I don't even know if I have the right to feel good about your attention. Maybe the attention I've received from you has been the result of my being a fraud.

I think I've always known I was a fraud. But, I hadn't attached any words to it until now. I never realized how much my conflict over attention has dominated everything I do, think, or say. Do you have any idea how momentous it is to be able to put words to these feelings that have plagued me for my entire life?! I suppose this is not a very positive thing to discover about myself, but it is ENORMOUSLY important to have figured out a lifelong, monumental conflict. At least I now know what has made things so difficult for me during all these years.

Can you imagine that all of this went through my mind within just a few minutes? So, now it feels like the only way I'm safe from dishonesty is not to communicate at all. BUT I am so pained from being alone that I can hardly exist. I'm so confused about everything I've done. I don't know what I should say, or do next with you, or anyone, or anything. So, for all the honest and "right" reasons (I think), I am now asking you whether I should even speak at this point. I don't know what I can or cannot tell you I feel—if I should, if I can, if, if, if, if. And, don't respond with "just let yourself feel whatever comes naturally and that will be right." Because, what comes naturally feels too horrendous.

Terry

4:07 P.M.

Oh Terry,

The amount of work you are doing is so incredible. I'm in awe of your abilities to self-reflect. I can feel the absolute turmoil, and the world, as you knew it, being turned upside down. But, the world you made for yourself needed shaking up because it was so damn restrictive, limiting, and judgmental.

Because of overwhelming experiences throughout your childhood, you never learned the other parts of "attention." The side that says, "Well that feels good, and I am proud of myself, too, and I'm happy others realize I've done something worthy, or good, or helpful." Attention was too fraught with all the dangerous, complicated, self-serving things. How could there be any good derived from the "getting of attention?" You never learned this, and now it seems impossible. But, because you haven't learned it, and because it seems impossible, doesn't make it so. It just speaks to a gap, albeit a HUGE gap, in your learning.

Can't you see what it cost you? By not talking to people about your feelings, you deprived yourself of a way to fill a need, a need that everyone has—to be recognized and cared for.

I think what you are saying is the following:

"I want you to pay attention to me, because when you do, it feels good. I don't understand how you can like ME, the me that is a fraud. I know that you do, but I CANNOT explain or make sense of this, because I don't feel like a likable person. Therefore, I must have fooled you into caring about me. And, I did this by exaggerating some issues. These caused you to attend to me. Without those issues, why would you care?"

232

Imagine, Terry, actually feeling good about being cared about. But you can't allow for that because you don't like so much of yourself. You simply can't imagine that despite all that you write, I still like you. It doesn't fit into your schema, and you try to make sense of it by debating yourself, making it impossible to believe that there isn't anything you could say or do that would make me stop caring about you. Even if you were completely and utterly happy, and had nothing to say in my office, even if you made something up, or were enraged at me, or tried to die. I might have lots of reactions and feelings to these things, but one of them would not be, "I better get out of this." And, because you feel so badly about yourself, the only explanation left is that you fooled me, and that you did so by making some smaller issues HUGE. At least that is your fear.

Living in a world inhabited only by yourself, while safe, is so damn empty and meaningless. If what comes naturally to you feels so horrendous, then together we will deal with it.

Cali

CHAPTER 24

A Sheep Among Wolves

April 2001

It would be a long while before I was out of the woods, but the cadence of insightfulness had begun to shift, leading us to a more promising clearing. Even if I didn't like what I first saw, I was much more comfortable with beginning to know myself, rather than continuing to live without explanations for my unhappiness.

The toxicities from Christmas had flushed from my body, and the poisons of my thoughts were being cleansed with the nourishment of healthier living. The effectiveness of anti-depressants continued to permeate the haze, and clarity emerged from the aggregate of months of hard work, both in and out of Dr. Joseph's office. Like snapping the sand out of a wet beach towel, the influx of "therapeutic moments" became an explosive flow of self-awareness.

"Being able to e-mail you is really helpful, Cali. I'm glad I was able to get it all down," I began, as I took a seat.

"That's great, Terry. I'm happy you were able to think things through and write to me. But, we still need to focus on working *inside* the office," Cali urged.

"I know," I said. "But, it didn't come to me until after I left here, and then I had a flood of thoughts."

"I'll take your thoughts any way I can," Cali smiled. "But, let's just pay attention to making it easier for you to talk to me face to face, okay?"

"Okay, I'll try," I replied.

"I think the work we are doing now is critical. Attention has always been fraught with such negative connotations for you. I want to help you see that needing attention is not inherently dishonest. But I think there is more to it than just trying to be the antithesis of your family," Cali suggested.

"What do you mean?"

"Not liking your appearance, or when others look at you, for example, suggests feelings that are very old. There is something about your disdain for drawing attention that's beyond trying to be the 'anti-family,'" Cali continued.

"Well, I don't see it."

"When was the first time you remember not liking how you looked?" Cali asked.

"I don't know. A long time ago," I obstinately replied, suspecting we were heading back to the dreaded "child-abuse-textbook-theories."

"Well, think about it," she persisted.

"I don't know, probably around the fourth grade," I answered after quickly scanning to the first unhappy years I could recall.

"*Ten years old again?*" Dr. Joseph remarked, as I was silently forced to begin digesting the "coincidence." "What do you remember feeling about your looks during that time?" she continued.

"That was when I began to dress differently. I remember feeling more comfortable in jeans and t-shirts, but at the same time, I hated looking like a tomboy," I answered.

"Wasn't that also right around the time Louis started sexually abusing you?" Cali asked, making her point under the guise of posing a question.

"Yes, but the way I dressed was *not* because of him. It was just the way I felt more comfortable," I insisted.

"So, you dressed that way, *even though* you didn't like how you looked?" Cali cocked her head, with a challenging raise of her eyebrows.

"Right," I defiantly answered.

"And, you dressed that way, *even though* you wanted to be accepted and have friends at school? Even though it made you feel different than the other girls and less popular?"

"Yeah," I replied with a lessening conviction.

"Do you *really* believe that how you dressed was random, and unrelated to the abuse, or anything else that was happening in your life at the time?"

"No," I answered, unable to continue denying the relevancy with a straight face—but wishing I could.

"Why is the connection between the abuse and how you felt as a child so difficult for you to acknowledge?"

Much like repeatedly referencing our "relationship," Dr. Joseph frequently integrated the word "abuse" into our conversations. She seized every opportunity to desensitize me to the concept we had been discussing.

"Because, again, it sounds like such an overplayed generalization for me to say that I was *'covering myself up because I was abused,'*" I sang with sarcasm. "It's so generic. Sort of along the lines of, 'tell me about your mother,'" I argued.

"But, just because the same consequences may be widespread among other abused children, doesn't mean you can't feel them, also," Cali explained. "Do you understand what I'm saying? It's important, Terry."

"I think so," I replied, suddenly feeling slightly emancipated from my paranoia with the terminology. It was the first time it occurred to me that legitimate reasons formed the basis for those generalizations. More importantly, Cali's comment marked the beginning of slowly permitting myself to *feel* some of those commonalities that occurred among abused children, without becoming the dramatist I had forever tried to elude.

"What else do you remember feeling when you were 10?" Cali continued.

"Very lonely and sad. It's frustrating to think back on my life during that time."

"Why?"

"Because I felt so stuck. I had no fucking privacy," I exclaimed.

"What do you mean?"

"Louis would listen in on my phone calls, and stare at me all the time. I was never allowed to lock the doors to my bedroom, or the bathroom. I used to keep the shower curtain closed for as long as possible so I could race to dry myself off behind it. Even as an adult, I catch myself rushing, and have to remind myself that it's different now; Louis is not going to walk in at any moment." The floodgates were bursting open, and a rapid momentum of memories began to pour out of me.

"What else do you remember?"

"Louis used to watch me. It drove me *crazy*. All the bedrooms were on the second floor, and mine was directly across from the banister. He used to stop on his way up the staircase and peak through the corner of the landing, and just watch me. I could see the top of his head, or the flicker of light off his glasses. He was like a goddamn stalker. I don't know *what* he was looking at. I was usually just doing my homework, or playing with my dollhouses."

"That sounds unbelievably sick, Terry."

"Yeah. He was a sick bastard." My face winced as though I had just taken a sip of sour milk. "Whenever I shut my bedroom door, I'd constantly catch glimpses of his eyes, looking through the space underneath it. One day I found a small hole drilled in the lower corner of the paneling on the door. I used to plug it up with a miniature bottle from my dollhouse. But, it kept *mysteriously* popping out, and I'd find it somewhere on my bedroom floor."

Cali sat quietly, careful not to interrupt the flow of my thoughts. I was so engrossed in the memories that it was as though she wasn't even in the room.

"It gets worse," I continued, narrating the horror movie playing behind my eyes. "He never wore clothes to bed or around the house. He used to "check" on me at night. He'd stop at my doorway and just stand there, naked, watching me in my bed. I would pretend to be asleep, but I could see him in the reflection of the mirror on my bureau. Some nights, I would keep count of the amount of times he kept returning. I remember lying there feeling so frustrated that he wouldn't just *go away*. Can you believe it was accepted as normal for him to walk around the house naked?"

"No, Terry, I can't. Where was everyone else? Where was your mother?"

"Sleeping, I guess. She used to play him up as such a great *father* for checking on me and being so protective. Looking back on it, I don't know *what* she was thinking," I sighed, still detesting the reference to him as my father.

"Did you ever tell your mother about the sexual abuse?"

"Yeah, when I was 13. I ran away to my father's house in California. While I was there, I wrote her a letter and told her what had been happening with Louis," I replied.

"Had you told your father about the abuse?" Cali asked.

"No. My father didn't know anything. I only told my stepmother. She was the one who helped me write the letter to my mother," I answered.

"Why didn't you tell your father? I don't understand," Cali squinted.

"I guess my stepmother feared that showing him the letter would incite a bloodbath."

"What did the letter say?"

"I told my mother about Louis touching me, and I reminded her of what happened the night she caught him in my bedroom. I told her how I felt about the showers, and a number of the other things," I answered, surprised by my candor and willingness to open the door to events formerly held captive by my fears of "playing the victim."

"What happened after she read your letter?"

"She called me at my father's house, and wanted to go over some things in excruciating detail. She kept focusing on whether or not Louis had intercourse with me."

"Did he?"

"No."

"Did he ever put his finger inside of you?"

"Yes. But, Cali, *I know*. I used to practice criminal law," I said, addressing her implication. We both knew that vaginal entry, even digitally, fell within the definition of rape. "There's no doubt it was repugnant, but it was *not* the equivalent of rape," I said unconvincingly.

The demon of minimization had reared its incongruous head again. But the process would no longer permit me to remain deafened to the absurdity of my own words.

"Are you okay talking to me about this now?" Cali asked softly, refraining from comment.

"Yeah, I guess," I ambivalently replied.

"What else was said during the phone call with your mother?"

"She forged ahead with a lot of questions about the specifics. I know she was desperate and in shock, but probably relieved in some way. I think if there had been intercourse, she would have had to face a much more difficult choice about leaving him. My mother was very dependent upon Louis, financially and emotionally, and probably terrified that her whole world had just crumbled."

"Did she end up leaving him?"

"Yes. She confronted him, and then they separated," I answered.

"How did that make you feel?"

"It was terrible, because it seemed like no matter what happened or where I was, I was miserable. Everything that I had been feeling for years caught up with me when I was living at my father's house. I had ulcers and was so reclusive that I hardly left my bedroom. I didn't make one friend during the entire time I was in California. Plus, I was looking more and more like a "tomboy"—which didn't help matters. After about six months, I flew back to visit my mother for a couple of weeks. That's when they decided that it was best for me to stay there, and live with her again."

"Who decided? What do you mean?" Cali looked confused.

"My father and stepmother spoke to my mother on the phone, and they all agreed," I explained.

"Why did they decide that?"

"Because, I was so miserable in California. I don't remember being too upset about their decision. In fact, I was relieved that the choice had been made for me. I was so happy to see my best friends and to be reunited with my mother. Until my twenties, I always thought of her as my best friend. But,

I still dreaded having to live with Louis again," I explained, knowing that I hadn't even scratched the surface of the events that had unfolded.

"What do you mean *'live with* Louis again'? I thought your mother separated from him and that he was gone?" Cali inquired, looking stupefied.

"He *was* gone—for a brief time," I began. "At first he denied everything I said in my letter. But soon he admitted to some physical contact with me. However, he said that *I* was the one who came *to him*. They went to marriage counseling and reconciled shortly afterwards."

"At *10 years old*, he claimed *you* were the perpetrator of the abuse?" Cali asked in disgust.

"Yeah," I answered, realizing that many of the factors I had glossed over for years were now becoming equally confusing to me.

"And, *knowing* what he had done to you, *they allowed you to live with him again?!*" Cali practically shouted in disbelief.

"Yeah. I suppose the touching was minimized because, it was not forcible rape," I answered, feeling an unfamiliar outrage arising inside of me. "The perception has always been that it wasn't that severe."

"Your perception or theirs?"

"Theirs, I suppose. I bought into it for a long time, too. Anyway, what's done is done," I said in my usual mode of self-containment.

"But what was done is *not* done, is it?" Cali asked.

"No, I guess not," I answered.

"Terry, *even if* you did go to him, *even if* you jumped on his lap naked, *even if* the touching was brief, *he* was the grown up, and *you* were the child. The fact that anyone diminished what happened to you, or held you in any way responsible, is contemptible. Do you see that?" Cali's eyes were filled with fury.

"Yes," I agreed, feeling a lifetime of self-condemnation dwindle to just a faint reservation in my heart of hearts.

"You mentioned last session that your mother caught Louis in your bedroom," Cali began. "What happened? How old were you?"

I could already feel the anxiety closing my throat. But a newfound freedom to speak was kicking down the doors that had previously vaulted in my memories.

"Around eight or nine, I think. Louis was naked and drunk. He woke me up, stood at the side of my bed, and told me to take my underpants off. I didn't want to and I started to cry. My mother must have heard the commotion, and came in."

"What did she do?"

"Louis had already left the room, and was stumbling down the hall, back to their bedroom where he passed out. She and I went downstairs and sat in the living room. I don't remember much more about that night. The next day Louis tried to be nice and helped me with a science project for school. He made a comment like, 'You sure caused a lot of trouble around here last night.' Other than the letter I wrote to my mother a few years later, no one mentioned that night again," I said, more astonished than ever that nothing had been done about it.

"That's incredible," Cali responded, clearly sharing my disgust. "How does it make you feel to talk about this?"

"Appalled. The more I think about it, the more pissed off I get that anyone was able to look the other way," I angrily replied, feeling the flame turn up on my simmering bitterness.

"Will you tell me what happened in the shower?"

For a moment, I contemplated not answering, and regretted that I had ever mentioned it. But, I felt an unfamiliar need to tell Dr. Joseph more. I was surprised that she had remembered my comment about the shower, given all that I had told her. As usual, she didn't let too many things get by her. I stomached the queasiness, and proceeded in the direction I knew to be in my best interest.

"He used to give me showers, and I hated it, because, of course, he always took his time with me," I answered, feeling nauseous as I heard the words come out of my mouth.

"How old were you when he was doing this?" Cali delicately asked.

"It happened until I was about 12," I continued.

"*Twelve*? Where was your mother during these showers?"

"I don't know," I stalled. The question was leading to an obvious conclusion.

"Just think on it for a moment," Cali asked with her patient style of unyielding persistence.

"Most of the time she was downstairs, cleaning up after dinner," I said, inching towards the unsettling reality.

"What was said before you took the shower? Put it in a context for me, Terry. What was going on?" Cali continued.

As though readying myself for a cliff dive, I shut my eyes and took a few slow, meditative breaths. "My mother would cheerfully say something like, 'Okay, go upstairs with your father and get cleaned up,' like it was a loving thing he was doing. It was never thought of as a big deal," I sighed, with my shoulders dropping in despair.

"Did *you* think it was a big deal?" Cali asked.

"Yes," I said, increasingly troubled by my own compliance.

"How did you feel going up those stairs?"

"I dreaded it."

"Why didn't you say 'no'?" Cali asked, highlighting the fearful atmosphere of the house.

"Because I *always* did as I was told, Cali," I said emphatically. I could feel the mounting resentment for being so herded as a child.

"What do you think would have happened if you did say 'no'?"

"I don't know. I never did," I whispered, still feeling the threat of questioning Louis' authority.

"Couldn't you tell your mother how you felt?"

"Not about that. She was the one telling me to go upstairs, like she was saying, 'go get in the car because daddy is going to take you to get an ice cream.' But she didn't know exactly what he was doing," I said, although increasingly baffled by the situation.

"Do you think your mother could've said 'no' to Louis about anything?" Cali asked, continuing to develop the climate of my childhood home.

"No. Well, yes, sometimes, but it came with grave consequences. They fought a lot."

"Did Louis ever hit your mother?"

"Yes, a number of times. That's one of my worst memories. Seeing her hit was much more painful than anything that happened to me."

"Where were you when Louis was hurting her?" Cali continued.

"One time, I was in bed. I heard them fighting downstairs. As usual, he was making vulgar threats like, 'I'll cut your tits off and shove them down your throat.' Lovely, huh?" I sarcastically commented, noting the lunacy. "I think he was drunk. He ordered her to get out of the house, and never come back. She pleaded with him not to make her leave her children behind. Well, *I* thought he could *really* force her to do that, and that she would be gone forever. So, I started crying at the top of the stairs. He stopped yelling and told her to 'Shut that kid up,' and allowed her to go up the stairs to comfort me. Then he left the house in a rage." The accrual of each elaboration began to reinforce Cali's theory that I had felt much more afraid and alone as a child than I had previously been willing to acknowledge. "As always, they made up the next day. He came

home with his ritual post-blow-out bagels and all kinds of good
breakfast stuff for us."

"Did you ever talk to your mother about how afraid you
felt?"

"No. I don't remember questioning her decisions until I
became much older," I said, startled at how sheepishly I had
behaved. I paused and looked across the room at Dr. Joseph.
The heaviness in my chest felt like it was crushing my lungs.
I was barely able to inhale. Vivid glimpses of terror were
scrolling past my eyes. I could see the expression on my
mother's face as Louis dragged her down the stairs by the hair,
leaving me in a trail of fear. I could hear the torturous sound of
her whimpers during the times I had stood outside their locked
bedroom door, and listened to her begging for him to stop,
praying she would soon emerge without being hurt.

"This must be very difficult to remember," Cali said,
picking up on my obvious distress.

"Yeah," I replied, with a disbelieving shake of my head.
"But Cali, I'm not sure I understand the purpose of elaborating
in this much detail," I wondered, feeling worn out by revisiting
each ordeal.

"Because, Terry, these are things that have clearly impacted
who you are and how you *feel* about yourself today. There is
a purpose to our discussions. I've learned over the years that,
for some people, it's therapeutic to talk about things until they
really feel them, rather than just remember them like some old
coat they wore," she explained. "Do you understand?"

"Yeah, I guess."

Cali's coat analogy was enormously effective. Sometimes it was the simplest statements that crystallized months of work. Flushing out more of the details had pivoted me in all different directions, and stirred me in ways I had never before experienced. For the first time, I was beginning to conceptualize the critical difference between talking *without* feeling it, and talking *with* feeling it.

"We have to end now, but I want you to give some thought to whether or not you still believe that you had any percentage of responsibility for the sexual abuse. And, before you answer, I want you to think about your 10-year-old niece, and if you would hold her *in any way* responsible under the same circumstances," Cali requested, as the session came to a close.

12:31 A.M.

Dear Cali,

I thought about what you asked me yesterday. Of course I wouldn't hold my niece, or any other child that age, responsible. And, yes, I am fully aware of the hypocrisy. But, just because I understand much more about the climate of my upbringing, and how I was affected, doesn't mean that I no longer hold myself partially responsible.

Overall, I grew up feeling loved and wanted. I don't ever specifically remember thinking, 'I am unprotected,' or 'I better go over there or Louis will hurt me.' So, it's still difficult for me to agree that I wasn't accountable for some of what happened.

I'm wondering what is so wrong with being responsible, anyway. Don't you agree there are exceptions, and that taking some responsibility is appropriate in some situations? Don't forget, I walked over to him.

Terry

7:13 P.M.

Terry,

Just because you don't remember THINKING, 'I am unprotected' in words, does not mean you didn't FEEL it on some level. It's far too scary for children to consciously admit that they don't feel safe. So, they create an illusion that they hold some control over what is happening to them. One way you avoided living in constant fear of Louis was to think that you had a choice, and were voluntarily walking over to him.

You cannot look at your feelings in a vacuum. You need to consider the entire context. This is why we've worked so hard to view the atmosphere in your house from every angle we could. We've looked at your loneliness, your thoughts of suicide as early as the fourth grade, and how you dressed like a tomboy. We factored in how you ran away because you were unable to stop the things that you dreaded and hated so much. And, how you did so, despite the fact that it was a time in your life when your friends meant everything to you.

We've looked at your age, Louis' age, the fighting you witnessed, how compliant you were, Louis' intimidation of your mother and her fear and dependence on him, how Louis stood naked in corners, stared at you, and even drilled a hole in your bedroom door. Then we put all this information together, and

250

hypothesized that you probably felt unprotected and unsafe in your home.

Oh Terry, there is nothing wrong with taking responsibility when you ARE responsible. There IS something wrong with taking responsibility in order to be the antithesis of others. There IS something wrong when you take responsibility in order to avoid feeling angry. There IS something wrong with taking responsibility because you feel like you deserve it, even when all things point to the fact that if it was anybody else in the universe, you would agree that they were not in the least responsible. How can you explain that?

I want you to think about what your sense of responsibility is all about. Could you possibly be holding onto this feeling NOT because you believe it anymore, but because it is so familiar, and you have ALWAYS told yourself that it's what you SHOULD feel?

Despite what you've said, I do believe it's easier for you to accept responsibility than to think through your feelings about the others involved and the atmosphere of your childhood.

Cali

"Let me ask you something, Terry. You said you knew what was happening on the easy chair with Louis was wrong. If you thought of your mother as your best friend, why didn't you tell her?" Dr. Joseph asked, beginning our next session.

"I can't remember exactly. I'm assuming it was because I felt too guilty for participating."

"Did you tell her how you felt about the showers?"

"No," I answered, wondering why Cali seemed to be asking what appeared to be such accusatory questions.

"Did you feel guilty about participating there?"

"No."

"Then, if you didn't feel guilty about participating in the showers, why didn't you tell her how you dreaded them?"

"Because, I never questioned the authority of the house."

"Why not?" Cali asked, spinning me around with perhaps one of the most compelling lines of questioning she had ever posed.

"Because," I breathlessly began, "I must have been too afraid to speak up." Suffocated by an avalanche of emotions, I suddenly realized that my fear and Louis' control over me were undeniable.

"*Must have been?*" Cali pushed.

"Okay. So, I was too afraid," I finally agreed. I could feel my dreaded desperation to just get the showering over with, as I stood there naked and vulnerable, just waiting for Louis to finish touching me, drying me.

"Your reasoning no longer makes sense, Terry. Despite all the things we've explored that demonstrate otherwise, you've held onto the belief that you had some sort of choice when you walked over to Louis because you were *not* in fear. But, your theory doesn't hold up. *We know* that you were intimidated and afraid. You *cannot* have it both ways," Cali persuasively concluded.

A response was hardly necessary. Months and months of grueling work converged into one of the most profound *therapeutic moments* I had ever experienced. Twenty-five years of self-condemnation began to give way to a new twist of logic. Believing that I had no choice no longer felt like just a cop out.

CHAPTER 25

Rings of the Past

May 2001

The sound of the security bells cut through me like a machete, axing the cables of an elevator. I dropped to the floor of the dressing room, covered in the disarray of clothing that fell from my arms. Unchained from the constraints of trying to live as the antithetical embodiment of *the victim*, I had begun to grant myself license to consider that there were legitimate connections between events during my childhood and my present feelings. However, I had not been prepared for this heightened awareness to invite an emotional ambush.

I could hear the women lining up outside the door, waiting to try on their clothes.

The simple chime that alerted sales personnel to the presence of customers catapulted me into a backwards spiral to the years I thought I had left behind. My debut into a new consciousness was going to delay the availability of my dressing room.

Installing the battery-operated doorbells throughout our house had been my idea. While Kurt was alive, I was so caught up in the daily management of his illness that I had passed off my dread of responding to him as the exhaustion from full-time care giving. What was left of Kurt's voice could not be heard from room to room. By gently pressing a button I attached to his wheelchair, the system was designed to replace his having to call out to me. Without fail, I internalized my agitation, and made immediate, poised appearances. From dangerous choking episodes to the more routine trips to the bathroom, composure was a prerequisite to being prepared to address the full range of his needs. I never knew what I was about to face.

The system was a perfect solution except for one lingering, unmet challenge. There wasn't a home health care improvisation in the universe that could manage the shell-shocked reaction of my reflexes. Almost two years after Kurt's death, I sat on the floor of a department store's dressing room, with tears of clarity streaming down my face. I had spent over two decades trying to tolerate a bell that wouldn't send shivers up my spine. The irony of it had moved back into my home with Kurt, in the form of a simple battery-operated doorbell attached to his wheelchair. The link seemed so patently obvious that I could hardly believe I had ever missed it.

As a child, reporting to the sound of a buzzer outside my bedroom door never struck me as unusual parenting. However, my adult perspective now cast a floodlight on the peculiarity. I was in elementary school when Louis wired the house. With the press of a button from the living room downstairs, I was signaled to report to him immediately. Typically, he wanted me to get him a drink, make him a sandwich, or change the television channel. Louis didn't like having to get up. I was aghast at the memory of his less frequent request—to get some lotion and give him a foot massage. Not hearing the buzzer because I was playing music in my room was an unacceptable excuse.

I pushed the heap of clothing aside and brought my knees to my chest. As though trying to contain an explosion of thought, I pressed my palms firmly against my forehead. "Of course," I thought to myself. Despite distinct memories of my rising resentment over having to militantly report to Louis, I never once recalled questioning his authority. The intimidation and fear were now even more glaringly obvious. I didn't stand a chance of adapting to a similar system with Kurt. Surely, Kurt wouldn't have agreed to the idea had he known its profound impact on me. But, even I wasn't aware that, in its own merciless way, history was repeating itself.

Given the horrors of Kurt's condition, the guilt over feeling sorry for myself about *any* of his care was overwhelming. I had been so mired down by my own self-imposed expectations that I never permitted myself the right to complain about forever being on call. But I would never again write off my reaction to the bells as an exaggerated response to something I *should* have been able to endure. Loving Kurt and dreading having to report to a buzzer were not mutually exclusive. The identical chimes used by the store became the catalyst to a life-altering epiphany: There had been a long history magnifying my feelings.

I took my hands off my face and glanced at the kaleidoscope of reflections off the dressing room mirrors. Typically, I would have made every attempt to bury the pain of my reaction behind a wall of composure, and continue on with my clothes shopping for upcoming job interviews. But ignoring my distress was no longer an option. The therapeutic process had primed me to be more receptive to my feelings, and fortified me with the tools to think them through to a new understanding.

Nothing was ever going to alleviate the sting of hearing those bells. But I was beginning to forgive myself for "not being strong enough" to overcome the unhappiness I felt over having to relive any part of my past. I was no longer on call. I was now an adult with a say over my own well-being, and over what I would subject myself to. With this understanding, I now had the power to affect whether or not history would ever be repeated again. I picked myself up off the floor, tried on every outfit I had carefully selected, and proudly walked out of there, ready to go back to work.

CHAPTER 26

The Swirl

May 2001

"I accepted a job," I cheerfully began. Weeks of interviewing were finally behind me.

"Where?" Cali asked, smiling back at the new person that took a seat in front of her, immediately sharing in my delight.

"I was introduced to one of the partners of an investment banking firm, and he interviewed me. I met with the remaining partners, and they offered me an associate position," I answered. "Truthfully, I can't believe they actually hired me."

"Why not?"

"Because, I'm an attorney. I don't have a clue what investment banking even is—never mind what job I took," I said, only half in jest.

"Please don't give me the 'I fooled another one' line, again. Maybe you have a lot to learn, but can't you just accept that someone saw you had potential?"

"Yeah, I suppose. Either that, or I'm a great sales person. But this time I think I may have over-sold myself," I replied, feeling the fear-of-failure monster take a seat next to me.

"Maybe you *are* skilled at selling," Cali responded, clearly irritated with my self-effacement. "Did you ever think that maybe your ability to sell yourself *is* your forte?"

"No," I answered. Even if I felt under-qualified, I had never looked at my ability to sell in that light before.

"I'm sure that the people who hired you weren't duped. Can't you just admit that these people believe you are capable of handling the job?"

"Yes," I replied, still uncomfortable with the immodesty.

"Do you feel ready to go back to work full-time?" Cali asked.

"I've been feeling better, and I think it's time I get back to things," I said. I had volunteered for a couple of non-profit organizations after the funeral. But I hadn't made any firm commitments to a career path since Kurt's death.

"What do you think has helped you feel better?" Cali asked, forcing me to face my fear of speaking optimistically. Overcoming my discomfort of articulating the positive things in my life was one of several approaches Cali took in addressing my resistance to admitting the process was working for me.

"I'm not feeling as depressed. I've been sleeping better, I'm working out, and feeling more energized," I answered, feeling the therapeutic value of listing the progress I had made.

"Sounds great. What else has helped you?"

"I don't feel as bad about myself for wanting attention, or for feeling self-pity at times. It has been relieving to know that I haven't been dishonest my whole life," I answered, less burdened.

"Do you think the anti-depressants have been helpful?"

Cali smugly asked, nailing me on the omission—which had not been inadvertent.

"Yes," I grinned, reluctantly conceding to how stubborn I had been during the years I refused to even consider taking medication. "Being able to come in here and talk to you has really helped, too. I know that you are within arm's reach, and that I have a safety net," I continued with a more serious tone.

"That's great, Terry. How do you feel about cutting down on our sessions now that you are going back to work full-time?" Cali asked.

"Well, that's definitely a problem. I don't feel ready to do that, but I'm going to be in the city every day and I don't know how I'm going to be able to make *any* appointments with you," I replied, noticing how comfortable I was with speaking more openly about my attachment to Dr. Joseph.

"I agree that we have more work to do. I promise you that we will figure it out. Maybe your boss will let you start early once a week, so you can leave a bit early and make it to my last appointment. I can also try to stay a little later every once in a while. I know it's not the same, but we could always set up an appointment over the telephone, too. Let's just see how it goes. We will find ways to make it work. Okay?"

"Okay," I answered, feeling a mix of anxiety about separating from the refuge of her office, and an excitement for the future that I hadn't felt in years.

Orientation went smoothly. Several weeks into the job, I was plugged back into the workforce. My days were occupied from the moment I opened my eyes and went for my pre-sunrise workout, to my collapse back into bed every night. I commuted into the city by train, feeling at home in the rush hour crowds of people traveling into the workday ahead. The learning curve was steep. But, over all, I was devouring the challenge with a clear mind, and a hunger to learn as much as possible. Everything was going along rather smoothly—until one morning, when I glanced out of my office window.

The red car was parked across from my office building, seven floors below. I dropped back into my chair, my eyes drowning in tears of overwhelming grief. Not only was it the identical year and make, it was the exact two-tone color of Kurt's car, long since retired to the dump. The fact that it was parked directly in front of my window, in the only handicapped space on the entire block, was the pinnacle of the apparition.

"It is just a car, it is just a car, it is just a car," I repeated to myself. But controlling the flow of my thoughts was like trying to take a drink from a fire hose, soaking me in a torrent of emotions. I couldn't understand why I was spiraling down into a vortex of pain and negativity. After all, it was only a car.

My telephone rang rather quickly, after Dr. Joseph answered the midnight page. "What's wrong?" she asked.

"I'm sorry to bother you so late, but I can't stop crying," I answered.

"What happened?"

"Nothing. I don't know. I just feel like dying," I whispered.

"Do you feel unsafe?"

"No. I just don't want to be alive. It's different than being on the verge of killing myself."

"I trust you to tell me if you feel at risk. Tell me why you don't want to be alive," Cali inquired.

"I don't know. A million reasons."

"Like what?"

"I don't know. It's just a swirl of things," I answered."

"'I don't know' is not acceptable, Terry. I want you to try and figure it out," Cali softly demanded.

"I can't. Everything feels like a part of everything else," I sighed, still trying to control my tears. My anxiety had painted me into a corner. Everything was coming at me in a blur. Cali waited in silence, pushing me to choke out the words.

"Maybe it's because I had a couple of really bizarre things happen at work today," I slowly began. "It started this morning when I saw the car that Kurt used to drive parked outside of my office building. It's very rare to see that model because Chrysler only made a limited number of them. Besides, they were all junkers. In fact, other than the one that Kurt owned, I don't think I've ever seen another one on the road. It was like a sense memory—you know, when you hear an old song that brings you back to a certain time. All I could feel was pain when I saw it," I began, still aching for him to reappear.

"What else happened?" Cali asked.

"Well, after I saw the car, I felt like I was suffocating. So, I took a walk to get some air. I stopped at the corner coffee shop, and while I was standing in line, the guy in front of me ordered a Mountain Dew. I couldn't believe it. That was Kurt's favorite soda and I don't think I've ever known anyone else that drank it, especially so early in the morning. Cali, it was a line for *coffee* and the guy orders that—and nothing else. No donut, no muffin, or *anything*. I could barely speak when it came time for me to give my order," I explained.

"That must have sent you reeling, Terry. How do you think that led to you wanting to die?" Cali asked.

"Because, by the time I went back to the office, I was still fighting back tears. Everything came crashing down on me at once."

"Well, obviously we need to talk about what 'everything' is. Don't you have an appointment tomorrow morning?"

"Yeah."

"Are you going to be safe until then?"

"Yeah, Cali, and I'm really glad I'm coming in," I replied, fearful that my days of feeling better were coming to an end.

"Did you get any sleep after we hung up last night?" Cali began.

"No, not really. My thoughts were racing," I answered.

"I want to talk more about the swirl you mentioned. You said that everything came crashing down on you after you returned to your office. Tell me more about what happened."

"Seeing the car, and then hearing that guy order the Mountain Dew, slammed me. I can't believe that Kurt is dead, and I just wanted to see him get out of his old car. Then it hit me that I'm 36 years old, and *starting all over again* at a new job, at a new life. I don't even know if I'm smart enough to do the work I was hired for, and if I fail, I don't have any back-up."

Did something happen at work that made you feel like you were going to lose your job?" she asked, in more serious tone.

"No. I just feel so expendable. It's only a matter of time before they find out I'm a fraud," I answered.

"Has anyone complained about your performance, or indicated that you aren't doing well?" Cali asked, highlighting that my worries were based on my own fears, not the responses of others.

"No," I answered.

"This reminds me of our talk several weeks ago when you told me that you over-sold yourself. Tell me, how are you a fraud *now*?"

"We've already gone over this, Cali."

"Do you think that because we talked about something once, or even twice, means you're *done*?" Cali said, smiling.

"No," I answered. There was no end to the number of times Cali insisted on combing through my feelings, seeking any opportunity to untangle my anxieties.

"Please explain it to me. I'm not sure I got it then, and I want to understand it better," she urged.

"I still agree that when I was hired, I was able to make a good impression. I've always had the ability to create the perception that I'm competent. But this is different," I explained. Prompted by Cali's dismissive grin at my habitually stubborn attempts to make a distinction, I continued. "Now I have to perform. I'm surrounded by bright people, and I'm definitely not as smart as they think I am."

"I see. So, they're very bright investment bankers, but after spending several weeks working closely with you, they're *still* not smart enough to know you tricked them?" Cali laughed. "Do you really think they would keep you around, and continue to pay you if they didn't think you were intelligent enough to do the job?"

"No," I confessed. Regardless of my answer, I was stuck. Cali had a way of drilling me with challenging questions, with a thought-provoking, disarming manner that made me hungry for more. As though she were building a case, her methodical line of questioning laid the groundwork for an undeniable perspective. Emotionally, I still *felt* like a fraud, but intellectually, I had to agree that how I was feeling no longer made sense. "But I still worry about being an imposter," I continued, struggling with the conflict.

"Why?"

"I don't know."

"Not good enough, Terry. Tell me, specifically. How are you an imposter? How are you *not* doing a good job?" Cali persisted.

I thought for a few moments, but realized I couldn't come up with one concrete example. "Well, so far I am doing a good job," I had to admit. "If anything, I do too much because I'm always worried that what I produce isn't good enough."

"This feels very early to me, Terry. Does it remind you of anything in your past?" Cali asked, digging deeper.

"Yeah, I guess I've always been this way, even when I was in high school," I said, slowly recalling a number of examples.

"Well, how did you do?"

"I got good grades. But good grades don't necessarily mean I'm smart," I answered. "The anxiety I've always felt about not doing enough is what motivated me to study harder. I guess that's a nice way to say I was neurotic," I joked.

"Let me guess, Terry. You graduated with honors in college and law school," Cali hammered away.

"Yeah, I did. But, like I said, that doesn't mean I'm smart," I repeated.

"So, graduating with honors was fraudulent and unrelated to your intelligence?" Cali asked sarcastically. "Sounds to me like you aren't tricking anybody. Why is it still so difficult for you to say something positive about yourself?"

"I don't know," I replied. Cali's disapproving expression immediately caused me to retract my prohibited response with an answer. "I guess because I don't want to sound conceited," I continued.

"Terry, you won't even admit that you were a good student. I have never once heard you speak about being good at anything unless it's under protest. Do you really think you run the risk of being conceited? Do you understand that there is a difference between conceit and pride?"

"I understand what you are saying. But I don't think I can ever be one of those people who is always relaxed and never bothered or insecure about losing their job, or the things that are important to them," I replied.

"Terry, people who never worry are usually either naive or arrogant, not secure. Being afraid of loss is part of living. It's not a sign of weakness," Cali stated, enlightening me with another perspective. "But, it's not black or white—either you are arrogant, and *never* worry about loss, *or* you are always insecure, and worry about loss all the time. I'm not suggesting you would ever stop worrying. But, you have to find a middle ground. Do you understand why I've been asking you all these questions?"

"Yes."

"Why? Explain it to me."

I often thought of Dr. Joseph as the "Master of Why." It was an exhausting approach, but it required *me* to articulate the answers, and forced me to think things through to a more thorough understanding. Despite the regularity of the exercise, I was continually drawn in to the challenge.

"You are trying to help me break things down, so I can see that there's no basis for my worries about work," I answered, once again realizing the value of "Why."

"Ah, you *do* understand. Do you see how easy it is to just make blanket statements like, 'I'm afraid I'm going to lose my job,' and remain stuck with those anxious feelings? It's the process, Terry. If you *talk* about it, you will understand things differently. That understanding may change how you are feeling and hopefully, help you feel less worried, and maybe even a lot better about yourself. This is worth repeating, because I really want you to hear this: It's okay to like yourself and recognize your strengths. Do you see this?"

"Yes, Cali. I get the point. But, it's not just about losing a job. All the feelings I had at work made me miss Kurt even more. I know I wouldn't feel nearly as anxious if he was still alive. Not having him in my life seems to magnify everything, and I hate it because my sense of happiness or security shouldn't be dependent on him, or whether I'm alone or not."

"Oh Terry, stop feeling badly for feeling something," Cali softly pleaded. "There is no such thing as 'I should or shouldn't' feel this way. None of that matters because *you* DO *feel it*. You keep acting like you're the strongest superego in town—with all the 'shoulds' and 'don'ts', as though you must always be in control of what you're feeling. I never understand why people say they shouldn't feel something. The fact is, they *are* feeling it, and *so that feeling* is what has to be dealt with."

"Well, *that feeling* is weakness, because I'm an adult and I should be able to take care of myself. But, the truth is that *I'm tired* of having to worry about everything all of the time," I sadly replied.

"Terry, depending on someone is *not* a weakness. Where did you get that idea?"

"I suppose I saw the evils of it when I was growing up. I just don't ever want to wind up like my mother when she was with Louis. She had to put up with so much shit because she was so dependent on him for everything—financially and emotionally. Her entire world crumbled after their divorce. I don't want my life to center around one person," I replied.

"I'm glad you are now able to recognize when your childhood is impacting the way you think as an adult," Cali remarked. "But, do you ever see yourself in that position?"

"No, I guess not."

"Don't you think there is a big difference between being controlled by someone like she was, and having someone care for you, and make you feel safe?" Cali asked.

"Yes," I replied. The distinction made sense to me.

"Just because Kurt's death has had a dramatic effect on your life doesn't mean you were completely dependent on him, or that your emotional security revolved around him. Did you ever think that if Kurt had *not* died, you would be filled up in ways that would make other things feel lighter? This does *not* mean you were too dependent, or that you based your entire existence on him. Do you understand what I'm saying?"

"I do," I replied, grasping the point.

The concept seemed relatively simple. But, as with many other insights, it often took that one-hundredth conversation to finally shift my understanding to a place that could not have occurred without all our previous work. I never considered that being filled up by having Kurt in my life would've given me a *baseline of happiness*, and that this need for him did *not* equate to over reliance. I never again felt the pain of losing him accompanied by my fears of dependency.

"What do you think happened at work that made you feel like you wanted to die?" Cali asked, continuing to chip away at "the swirl."

"I was anxious about not being able to make it and then going bankrupt, and having to deal with being alone and miserable every day of my life," I answered.

"Do you see the pattern here? That "swirl" causes you so much anxiety that you immediately jump to your escape route of dying without first thinking through what you are so afraid of. Unless we continue to figure out what fears and anxieties comprise that swirl, you will always keep jumping to the dying part. Do you see this?"

"Yeah," I answered. "But, I can't do it, Cali. I understand how breaking it down helped me to look at what happened at work. But the rest is too overwhelming. There's so much going on in my head and it all blends together. All I know is that I'm unbelievably anxious."

"I suspect that much of your anxiety is because you are so mad that Kurt isn't around anymore to take care of you. And there is nothing wrong with wishing for this. You have a right to feel angry about it. But, suppressing this anger will continue to make you feel anxious. Why don't you ever seem mad about anything that has happened to you? You're always so damn composed."

"I *am* angry about things," I said calmly.

"*This* is you being angry?" Cali asked, raising her eyebrows.

"Yeah. Usually, when I get *really* mad, I implode and keep to myself. I'm not comfortable flying off the handle. Just because I'm angry doesn't mean I have to scream and yell."

"I'm not suggesting you scream and yell, however that might be a bit more relieving than swallowing it all. Do you realize that when many people get angry they *EXplode, not implode?*" Cali asked.

"Yes," I answered, never really having given it a thought before. "But I grew up in a volatile house, and I don't have much tolerance for explosive tempers. Remember how hard it was for me to adjust to Kurt's speech because he always sounded angry? Plus, I think that once you raise your voice, no one really listens to you anyway. You just wind up becoming more frustrated and pissed off. I'd rather be more prudent about how I act," I explained.

"Prudent. Well, that sounds just like you, Terry. But, don't you ever *just feel something* without intellectualizing about it first? Without being so prudent?" Cali pushed.

"I guess not. It's always been an instinct for me to be prepared. It's how I feel most comfortable. I hate hysteria, and I don't want to be pushed into a tantrum just for the sake of expressing some anger," I quipped.

"Terry, we aren't *manufacturing* anger. Nor are we talking about anger for the sake of expressing it. We're *addressing* it together. There is a purpose to expressing your feelings out loud—and *feeling* them. You know, that "old coat" theory? At the very least, you don't have to carry it alone. Talking about how you're feeling is better than trying to manage it yourself," Cali explained. "I think a lot of your anxiety is the result of being so prudent, and internalizing your anger along with the fears that fuel it."

"I can see that, but my composure is a knee jerk reaction. It's almost like the more angry I become, the more calm I become. It's the only control I've had in order to stay afloat—

with others, as well as myself. Staying as busy as possible helps, too. It keeps me distracted. The only problem is when I can't keep the pace going."

"Dealing with "the swirl" by running yourself into the ground may be okay for the moment, but there is a down side to it. Do you realize that most people don't have to live trying to distract themselves all day?" Cali pointed out.

"Truthfully, I don't think I've ever thought about that before," I replied, astounded that any other way of living through each of my days had *never* occurred to me.

"I want you to learn that pausing for a moment and feeling things, even intensely hard things, is survivable," she continued.

"But, I'd rather wait until I'm alone to feel rage. I don't know if I'm capable of being with anyone without keeping up some appearances."

"I understand how hard it is for you to be wide open with me about your anger, and to be so known. But, waiting until you are alone to feel mad stinks for both of us. I mean, why would you ever share being pissed off with your therapist?" Cali said, smiling. "Did you ever think that it is the very stopping of these feelings that led to your thoughts of suicide and what happened at Christmas?" she asked, returning to a more serious tone.

"No, but I think I'm beginning to understand it now," I answered.

"I want to make your old solutions so impossible that you use our relationship, and others, to help you look at the feelings you've found so unbearable. As you talk about the 'stuff beneath' and come to understand it, you will have so much more of a say about how things hit you, and when," Cali optimistically explained. "Don't let your past dictate your life, Terry. *There is a difference between passion and hysteria.* You just don't know this yet, but it's something I can teach you."

The web of intersecting roads that Dr. Joseph and I had charted over the course of almost two years had begun to converge. Despite the recurrent tug and pull over accepting new perspectives, we refined what had become our routine dance, as my initial, stubborn oppositions often learned to follow the rhythms of her tenacious lead. Our rapport had become forgiving enough to tolerate the expected tussles and missteps along the way. Although many ideas were not yet on board, our work continued to focus on the roadblocks to my destination of emotional comfort. The remaining therapeutic lessons were the bulldozer.

CHAPTER 27

Introducing You to Yourself

June 2001

Dr. Joseph stared back at me in silence.

"Are you going to say something?" I asked.

"Are *you*?"

Ten seconds into the session, and we were already doing our tango.

"Come on, Cali," I pleaded. She maintained her stare. Clearly, she was not going to take the lead. "What don't you want to talk about?" I mockingly asked.

"Hmmm. There is so much to choose from," Cali smiled, glancing towards the ceiling as she tapped her fingers in deliberation. "Of all the things we covered last session, which is the thing *you* least want to talk about?"

"Probably Kurt," I answered. "So, let's start with him," I said quickly, beating her to the punch.

Cali beamed, clearly pleased with herself.

"I am *all* DONE with him being dead. Game over. You know?" I sighed, bringing us back to my ever-present sadness. "I'm ready for him to come back now," I continued, as though my announcement allowed for his return.

"Oh Terry, don't you see that this is all part of the grieving process? You numbed yourself out for so long after Kurt's funeral that it's almost like you just started feeling everything you needed to feel two years ago. All you did was delay it," Cali explained.

"Yeah, I suppose so," I said. "My soul is lonely. But, it's not because I lack company. In fact, it's made even worse by constantly being surrounded by couples that seem to have so many of the things I lost. Painful envy is a big part of 'the swirl' and I *hate* feeling it."

"I'm glad to see that you're learning to break down your swirl of feelings. What do you mean by 'painful envy'?" Cali asked.

"I mean exactly what it says: Feeling envy about what others have is painful to me. It's very confusing because I want people around me to be happy. But, sometimes, I don't know whether I hate them, or wish them well," I explained. "It's just wrong to feel this way."

"Why do you think it's wrong? Who wouldn't feel pain if they saw others with what they wish they had? And, it's not either-or. You can want others to be happy *and* still feel pained. You can have both emotions at the same time. Why are you so hard on yourself for everything you feel?" Cali asked.

"I don't know. It feels selfish, or mean, or something," I began. "I just wasn't expecting to feel so down again. I was feeling better enough to get a great job, and re-start my life in a lot of different ways. Except for what happened the other day at work, I thought I was doing pretty well overall."

"But, you *are* doing better, Terry. All of these emotions are part of the grieving process. As you begin to really *live* your life, you're going to have a whole range of feelings," Cali explained.

"Remember when you told me that thinking and feeling this much was a gift? Well, right now it feels like a curse."

"What do you mean?" Cali curiously asked.

"Lately, I've noticed that my *gift* won't allow me the peace of knowing who I am. I don't know what's honest and what's not anymore," I said.

"I still don't understand. Explain it to me."

"I've been so used to keeping up appearances that now, when I'm optimistic with you, or with others, I don't know if it's a facade, or a short phase. But, when I'm negative, then I don't know if *that's* truthful either. It's as though either way, I don't know what to do or say anymore. Do you see why I want to return my gift?" I said miserably.

"Yes, I can see that. But, the confusion is, I'm sorry to say, a natural part of the process."

"So, this is a good thing?" I squinted.

"Yes. Because all you've believed about yourself needed to be shaken up," Cali began. "Deconstructing your cemented beliefs was the first step. You've always thought of yourself as a sham, or a fraud, or that you were born a loser who fooled us all. And you've been given a lot of opportunities to prove these tenets. However, I want to point out to you that, by looking to prove them, you've also *failed to DIS-prove the opposite*. So now you are stuck in this amazing bind—who or what to believe," she explained.

"So, how am I supposed to deal with the confusion?"

"You'll need to become reacquainted with yourself. Hopefully, you will rediscover who you are, and see what others, including me, see, and what that 'overactive' mind of yours has intuited and explored—and maybe even like yourself."

"Psychological Frankenstein," I jested.

"Yes, Terry. But, just because you think you've had monstrous thoughts and feelings, doesn't make you one. *I want to introduce you to yourself.* And, I will continue to search for ways to show you what I see—an honest, good person who has been willing to strip down and allow a search despite all the discomfort, shame, guilt, and terror that it entails."

"But how do you know this? How do you *really* know that I'm a good person?" I asked, desperately hoping for some form of final proof.

"*Because I know you,*" Cali answered.

It was a simple answer, but it rendered me speechless. Her words swung across the room like a sword, slicing through the noose around my rationale that I was loser. Even the pull of my poorest self-image could not refute that Cali *knew* me better than anyone ever had in my entire life. I trusted and respected her, and there was no way to dismiss her opinion as one that had been based upon my creation of appearances. Freed from the gallows of believing that I was an unknown, unlikable outsider, it was time for me to begin getting to know myself.

2:27 A.M.

Cali,

I've had a swirl of grief on the loose for days now. You encouraged me to just feel whatever I'm feeling, and I've remained so terribly confused. So, I thought it would be helpful if I just wrote everything I'm thinking out—even if it sounds terribly negative—so that you can see where my thoughts have been taking me.

I don't want to love anyone, and I don't want anyone loving me. I don't want to be with anyone. But I don't want to be alone anymore. I don't want to long for feeling good with someone else, in a way that I just can't have. I don't ever want to sleep with anyone again. But I don't want to sleep alone. I don't want to look at others and always be reminded that my husband is dead, and I am where I am.

I don't want to have to try so hard to want to live, to like being alive, or to just be comfortable. I don't want to see that I am never satisfied, that I can't appreciate what I have, or who I have, and just be a normal, somewhat contented person. I don't want to have to struggle through one more day of trying to manage and rebuild my life.

I don't ever want to be dependent on anyone. But, I don't want to always have to rely on myself to keep it all going— emotionally, financially, everything. I don't want to have to rebuild a career. I don't want to go into another job, trying to make it, trying, trying, and trying all the time to make people like me, or want me around. None of this happens for me without my having to fight, and fight, and fight for it.

I don't want to remember things the way I remember them. My conscience haunts me so badly that I can't even let my memories of Kurt be good ones. Instead, it's all the mistakes, all the bullshit, all the cracks that we fell through.

I don't want to always have to be so fucking rational, and be the person that everyone thinks I am. I'm tired of trying to be strong or sensible. I don't want to have to face the reality that I can't afford to be any other way. Because no one is going to take care of me, or be there for me to lean on when I just want to take a break. Just be able to stop, not worry, and know that I've got someone at my back so I can just relax for one minute, one second, one anything.

I don't want to have a family of my own. But I want to have a family of my own. I never want to have to take care of anyone again, or feel stuck, or love so much that I'm so vulnerable again. But I want to have children, and I don't want to live this life without the experience of caring for them. I don't want to face that I am at an age where it is now or never, and if I choose never, I am doomed to a solitude that is irreversible. I just don't want to give a shit about any of it, and I'm tired of carrying it alone.

I don't want to be a continual walking oxymoron—needing the things that I don't want to need, wanting the things I don't want. I never have just one consistent thought or belief. There always has to be a thousand different angles and a non-stop, relentless swirl of thoughts without being able to JUST BE— just be one thing, one way, or just know one thing, anything, without so much turmoil, so much preparation, deliberation, and consideration of every possibility. I can't even get away from myself for a minute and it feels like it won't, I won't, ever be good enough.

I know we talked about expecting the confusion. But I still don't understand how I can go from feeling so much better to having this downslide. Why are my feelings so volatile? I suppose I should just be grateful for the few hours of feeling good, but the downer time makes it seem like the happiness will always be fleeting—a dangling carrot, so to speak. It makes me terrified to feel hopeful, because when things don't work out for me, I will come crumbling down again. I'm afraid to discuss better periods of time because then they'll disappear and it will hurt even more when it does fade away. Why can't I just catch a break?

Terry

3:03 P.M.

Dear Terry,

In answer to your question, you (and I) caught a break when you woke up from your suicide attempt after Christmas. I will not allow you to believe that you would be any better off if you didn't hope, because hoping is part of living, and living is better than walking around with deadened feelings.

The question about your emotional volatility is an excellent one—suggesting you feel UP as well as down! A few months ago, you doubted even a moment of respite. First, it is important that you FEEL good. You need to remind yourself that you have come so far from Christmas Day when change never seemed possible. But we aren't going to settle for just moments, or even hours of feeling better.

I'm sorry you are feeling badly. It was bound to happen, though. Depression has a course that it follows. And I know it's hard for you to hold onto, but lately, you've been more available, feeling slight relief, and even some hope. The fact that you have been able to feel that way is the good news.

However, as with most illnesses, recovery is never without steps forward and backward.

It's possible for opposite emotions to both accurately reflect the way you feel. You can feel hopeful and scared at the same time. You can feel happy or optimistic, and still hold onto some healthy skepticism. You can't stop the guilt, or the loneliness, or the loss if you want to feel joy, connection, and love—if you want that peace you say you do. <u>Peace doesn't come from NOT feeling, it comes from being able to handle the feelings.</u>

Because of your past experiences, you're working from the premise that feeling badly is who you are, and feeling good is fleeting. However, can you imagine the possibility that feeling good could be who you are, and feeling badly would be fleeting? We have to trash that notion you hold onto. Damn the safety it provides you—it isn't working.

I know that feelings of depression and loneliness continue for you, grow worse, recede, grow worse and so on. You have to tell me when they feel unmanageable so we can work harder to find ways that help you feel better. We will continue to figure out past experiences, present choices, and future possibilities. Just don't stop feeling. Can't you tell that you are ever so much more alive?

You are now ready to take risks. I wish I could promise you that hope and joy won't disappear, but they will, and it will hurt. And, I will be there to remind you that you are human, and that the good feelings you allowed yourself to risk feeling will also return. Pain is temporary and those painful feelings, will fade, too. Steps forwards and backwards—that is how it is. You played it safe for too long. Or, rather what you thought was safe, and it cost you so damn much.

Cali

Our work continued over the following weeks with a focus on
exploring the components of my confusion and "the swirl."
My journey gained speed as I entered a vortex of introspection.
Like the creation of a musical composition, each session was
devoted to refining another piece, until the soundness of the
verse could be heard and felt. My feelings, standing alone,
started to become understandable, but it was difficult to
conceptualize them as a whole until I pieced them together into
one flowing melody. One summer morning, I finally heard the
music.

9:01 A.M.

Cali,

*You know how you keep telling me that sometimes it takes
saying things a hundred times until something clicks? Well, it
happened when I was at work this morning.*

*My boss started in with his usual, early morning task
mastering. I was hired to become an associate in the firm,
but lately, he's been stepping over the line by asking me to
clean up after him. I've been tolerating his behavior by trying
to convince myself that it's part of the dues I have to pay as
newcomer in the company.*

*However, today I noticed that I've been pre-empting his
demands by anticipating what he is going to ask for, and then
doing it before he asks. I even noticed that I interrupt him, and
try to beat him to his next sentence, and offer to do these things
before he even has the chance to finish. But, today it struck me
differently, and I realized why I've been doing this. It's because
I would rather be the one who is deciding to do all this bullshit
work—making it MY choice, rather than his orders.*

It immediately reminded me of what we talked about when I walked over to Louis on his easy chair, and the "few" seconds after I stopped fighting him. Do you remember how I said that walking over was my choice, and that those seconds in between pushing his hands away and succumbing to his touching me, made it my fault? I always held onto the belief that I had the control. Because, as you've suggested, if I faced the fact that it wasn't really my choice, then I would have had to deal with being fearful, oppressed, forced or whatever.

I got the same feeling this morning. I realized that this "pre-empting" under the guise of making my own decisions is something I do in order to avoid feeling that I am under someone's else's control. When I'm at work, I would rather feel like it's my choice than deal with the anger and feelings after I'm ordered to do something.

The main point is that, as reluctant as I will probably be to admit this later, I finally understood the importance of looking at the context around Louis. It makes a lot more sense. You can get up off the floor now.

Terry

5:28 P.M.:

Dear Terry,

It isn't often that I find myself absolutely at a loss for words, but your e-mail left me happily speechless. I think you just found a way to begin to forgive yourself for something that you unfairly blamed yourself, for a long, long time! And, you are right. It has been our talking, and going over this 247 times, and the remarkableness of it clicking the 248th time.

Do you remember when we first approached the sexual abuse?
You were so damn reluctant. You didn't want anything to be a
big deal, and you said you already knew everything there was
to know about it, because you had thought it through so much
on your own. WOW Terry, you just put your toe in a HUGE
ocean and said, "Wait a minute. During those few seconds,
I made it MINE in order to avoid feeling like I was under
somebody's control. And it was easier for it to be MINE than to
feel what must have really been going on during that time." Oh
Terry, do you feel it all? Do you feel all of the ramifications?

Cali

CHAPTER 28

Quotas

August 2001

Not being much of a gambler, I continued the struggle to acclimate myself to life's crapshoot. I had become so accustomed to tolerating the risks by not even playing that embracing each meaningful relationship began to feel like my first anxious toss of the dice. As weeks passed, my willingness to take the chances inherent to being with others was on the increase. But, no matter how adept I thought I had become at calculating the odds, I still found myself battling waves of panic whenever I fully realized the stakes.

"I'm sorry to bother you while you're at home. I tried to wait until I came in, but I just can't stop this massive anxiety attack I've been having all afternoon," I began, my heart pounding with the turmoil over having Dr. Joseph paged.

"It's okay, Terry. Tell me what's happening," Cali inquired.

"I don't know. I probably shouldn't have called," I replied, unable to conceal the anguish of my debate.

"What do you mean? Are you okay?" she asked with immediate concern.

"Yeah, I guess so. But, you probably just got in from working all day, and now I wish I hadn't called you."

"Really Terry, it's okay."

"But, it's not like I'm on the verge of killing myself," I nervously confessed, fearing her haste upon learning that things weren't grave enough to warrant calling.

"Okay, we've established that," Cali almost dismissively responded, startling me with how undisturbed she seemed by the level of the urgency.

Although subtle, her response was one of the most profound therapeutic moments I had ever experienced. I never imagined that divulging anything short of a life-threatening crisis would justify what I had assumed to be an unacceptable imposition. And, oftentimes, it was this very internalization that led to perilous levels of loneliness and depression. To my relief, her reaction began to eliminate my inclination to continue suffering through those periods of time alone.

"What's up? What's going on?" she persisted.

I paused, stuck in the dilemma of how to answer.

"What, Terry? Tell me."

"If I tell you, I just don't want you to insist that I take anti-anxiety meds."

"I would never *insist* that you do anything. Everything, *everything*, is open to discussion. Is this not clear from all of our work together?"

"No, it's clear," I agreed. "I guess I didn't think it through. But maybe I should've waited until tomorrow."

"Terry, I trust you to tell me what you need. You don't have to be hanging from a cliff to have me paged. I know you wouldn't have called unless you had to. What happened tonight?" she reassuringly asked.

"I don't know. Well, I do know, but even if I talk to you about it, nothing can be changed," I choked, sinking deeper into the quicksand of my fears.

"Oh Terry, even if it were true that nothing could be changed through the talking—which you know I wholeheartedly disagree with—sometimes it's helpful, just so you don't have to be alone with how you're feeling," Cali explained. "What is it?"

Heat surged through the tunnels of every blood vessel in my face as I braved the answer. *"I'm afraid I'm going to lose you,"* I confessed.

"How would you lose me?"

"Because, once I relax about you, I know you're going to die." Suddenly, the extent of my terror crystallized. "As soon as I let my guard down with Kurt, we got the diagnosis that he had ALS. *I'm not kidding.* Kurt and I had just had a heart-to-heart talk a couple of nights before, and any reservations I had about marrying him finally faded away. Pretty ironic, huh? *Two* fucking days after I let myself stop worrying about losing him. I just can't afford to relax, Cali. I couldn't weather that kind of loss again," I explained, no longer able to contain the flow of tears now soaking my cheeks.

"Oh Terry, given what has happened to the people you've loved and trusted, it makes perfect sense that you would fear that happening to me, too. Of course, I can't promise you I will *never* die. But I am young and healthy, and I can promise you that, as long as I'm alive, I won't turn away from you."

"How can you say that? Don't you think, at some point, you will have had enough of me? Aren't you getting tired of thinking ahead of me, around me, through me?"

"Have enough? What does that mean? That I will send you on your way before you're ready to go? Do you think I would do that to you? Our relationship, like all others worth having, will have its moments of disappointment and misunderstanding. But have we ever failed to figure something out?"

"No, I suppose not," I replied. "But, I'm trying not to get too used to any of this."

"Terry, because of your past, you are seeking an insurance policy against pain. But, what you are actually insuring is that you *will* feel what you seek to avoid—the pain of being alone. You have to risk loss in order to have the good feelings from being in relationships."

"I know, Cali. But it doesn't stop the panic that keeps coming over me every time I think about losing you—which is constantly, lately. I'm afraid I'm using up your energy, which I know I will continue to need."

"Do you think there is *some kind of quota* on the number of times you can come to me?"

"Well, yeah," I answered, never having questioned what I thought was the obvious.

"Why? What would make you feel that way?" Cali asked, sincerely perplexed.

"Because, people get worn out, Cali. It's only a matter of time before they end up bailing. I mean, in all fairness, you can't blame them. How can I expect anyone to *not* become drained or burdened by me?"

"Because, when you care about someone, there is no such thing as a quota. I'm not going to suddenly become drained. I might be tired, or unavailable, but we would come up with another time to talk. And if you just couldn't wait, you would tell me, and we would work it out. It would *not* be because I was tired of *you*. Do you understand?"

"Yeah, I guess so. There are definitely people I'm close to, who have always been there for me. But I've had shit going on in my life for years now, and I'm just afraid that the time will come when they are done with me."

"Has this been your experience before?"

"I don't know."

"Think about it, Terry. Who did you talk to when you were little?"

"Well, my father was gone. I usually talked to my mother. I felt very close to her, and we spoke about almost everything. But, I remember feeling frustrated at times, because I often felt that, no matter who I talked to, as soon as I had poured my guts out, it was time to move on," I responded, immediately struck by the lateness of the hour, and the fear that the same thing was about to occur at any moment with Cali.

"That must have been terribly difficult, and left you feeling so alone," Cali sympathized. Surprisingly reassured by her willingness to continue, it was apparent to me that history was not going to repeat itself.

"Yeah. Well, actually, I don't remember thinking 'This is terribly difficult, and I'm all alone,'" I said, instantly cringing at my own response.

"Stop it, Terry. Don't be so literal. How much time have we spent talking about feeling things, even if you didn't think them in words?" Cali admonished.

"More than enough," I conceded. "I think I've always been overly sensitive because of the perpetual crises when I was growing up. At some point, people get saturated, no one takes you seriously, and they just don't want to hear it anymore. It's very easy to cross the line and become an imposition."

"Talking to you is not an imposition, Terry. If it were, I would say so. You have to trust me to be able to take care of myself. Okay?"

"Yeah. I believe you, Cali. I really do. But it's still very difficult for me to accept that you're for real."

"Well, I *am* for real, and I want to talk to you about this more when we meet."

"I don't doubt it," I managed to light-heartedly joke, feeling the anxiety begin to diminish along with my regret that I had called.

"I've been doing a lot of thinking since our phone conversation the other night," I said, beginning our session. "I've been wondering about something and I wanted to ask you."

"Sure. What is it?" Cali asked.

"Sometimes you surprise me with your responses. It's like I never know what to anticipate because you always seem to have this poker face," I explained.

"Really? When have you been surprised?"

"I don't know. Maybe, when I'm being stubborn. But, usually, I've thought about it when you surprise me by being kind or patient when I assume you're going to respond otherwise. I don't know. I can't think of anything specific. It's just that I've noticed how I often misjudge what you're feeling—good or bad—and I can never figure out what you're really thinking."

"Well, that 'poker face' is very purposeful, Terry. Because, if I started to emote the way I feel, the work would be about me and my feelings, rather than about you. You would start to watch me, or try to take care of me by not wanting me to be upset, or angry, or anything uncomfortable. Do you understand?"

"Yeah."

"And I never want you to start feeling like you have to act or feel a certain way in order to protect me. I want you to be you, and feel all the things you feel, okay?"

"Yes," I answered, once again reminded of the focus of therapy.

"And I'm very glad you asked. Please talk to me about these things. You don't have to go home and wonder about them alone, okay?

"Yes," I replied.

"So, tell me how you've been feeling since our telephone call."

"I felt a lot better after I hung up, but I still have this overwhelming anxiety."

"What are you anxious about?" Cali asked.

"Because I haven't allowed myself to need someone like this since Kurt, and I couldn't survive another loss like that," I explained. "As soon as I let myself feel with abandon, I nose-dived."

"However, as you pointed out, the other end of the spectrum was the 'abandoned' joy you got to feel with Kurt. And you *will* have it again, Terry."

"But how do you know that? It's almost impossible for me to believe that I won't keep winding up alone. This is where I live. With the exception of Kurt, this is where I've *always* lived," I explained.

"But, if Kurt was an exception, what makes you think there won't be others? I don't think it's a coincidence that some of your fears about loss are starting to surface more profoundly right now. We're heading into the beginning of fall, and I think you should expect that the anniversary of Kurt's death next month will bring out a lot of painful emotions," Cali pointed out.

"I know this time of year is tough," I acknowledged. "But the bottom has dropped out more times than I care to count. I just wish I could make a plan. But how can I ever make a plan for you dying, or changing your mind, or becoming drained?"

"I understand the bottom has dropped out on you many times before, but you are alive today—thinking and feeling again. The plan isn't complicated, Terry. The plan is to trust me, to know that I care, and *if* the bottom should ever drop out again, to know that you won't be alone. *You don't need a plan for me dying.* You need a plan to figure out *how you are going to LIVE in this relationship.*"

"Okay," I responded, stunned by the notion. Another therapeutic lesson was added to the emotional score card. "But it feels like the approaching anniversary of Kurt's death is feeding my anxieties. It makes it even harder to believe you are for real," I continued.

"Part of having relationships is trusting. I think your turmoil over whether or not I'm for real is another way of saying, 'Can you be trusted, Cali?' You simply can't believe that I won't disappear, or die, or that you don't have to take care of me in order for me to continue caring about you."

"I agree," I admitted. "It *is* hard to believe. Regardless of what I know intellectually, emotionally, I'm still gun shy."

"Of course, you're scared. The important thing now is what you do with that fear. In the past you've tried to drug it away, and when that failed—because it *has* to fail—you tried to kill yourself. Fear diminishes pleasure, Terry. Imagine how it limits joy, being filled or touched by the feelings others send your way."

"So, how do I plan for *having* people, not *losing* people?" I asked.

Cali smiled. "First, you have to deal with the roadblocks, and those are about the losses you've suffered from being dependent and needy of people who either had emotional limitations, or left you. You have to *feel* all the feelings those losses have brought."

"Isn't that what I'm already doing?"

"Yes, you are. But, somehow, I think you've believed that you deserved these losses in some way because of the person you are—by wanting them too much—as if wanting has a limit. I want you to continue dealing with all of these things so you can make room for knowing the person that I know—the parts of you that are strong, insightful, determined, funny, honest," Cali paused, "and stubborn. That can be a virtue, too," she grinned.

"I'm trying, Cali. But it seems that the 'monsters of fear and doubt' keep rearing their heads, and I just can't seem to hold onto more optimistic beliefs long enough."

"One of the first steps is to know this fear, and part of feeling it is knowing it. The more you know it, the less power it will have over you and your future relationships."

"I know that not having happiness, because of the fear of losing it, or not having a person, because of the fear of losing him or her, is not what I want, but it's not that easy."

"I realize how difficult it is for you. You just have to trust yourself. Right now, you might not be able to understand this, but I do, and for now, that is enough because I will guide you until you can be on your own."

"I hate the fear, Cali. I really want to be able to relax again, but other than with Kurt, my mind has yet to work that way."

"We'll keep working on it, Terry—together. And I know you are worrying about imposing, or my getting tired or bored. I want you to know that just because you spoke to me on the telephone the other night, or came into the office today, you can still need me tomorrow. I am not worn out, and you have not used up your quota."

I soon accepted that I had been traveling throughout my life on a freight train filled with a personal gang of monsters—monsters of loneliness, anxiety, fear and destructive self-images. With an increasingly receptive stance, each new understanding unloaded another unwelcome passenger, making room for the new companions on my journey.

During the ensuing weeks, the fruits of our work ripened into a new self-awareness. Inner strength cracked open with the birth of growing confidence. Dr. Joseph was right: As I began to feel differently about myself, I was able to take risks with others I had rarely dared before. Life was indeed a crapshoot, but this time the odds were in my favor. Louis would be my next stop.

CHAPTER 29

Pampering

September 2001

With less than two weeks left for him to live, I neared the fulfillment of a twenty-two-year fantasy. News had traveled fast through the six-plus decades of Louis' predatory existence. Stomach cancer was soon to vindicate the trail of victims he left behind. Anxious that I would miss the opportunity to take a fearless and final look into his menacing eyes, I hurriedly cut into the front of the line before death's door. His address scribbled on a scrap paper in my pocket, I took myself out of my body and started the car. The eighty-mile ride back to my childhood would only take moments.

The sun began to peek over the horizon as I pulled into the vacant, sleeping center of the small town that seemed most characteristic of the quaintness of Cape Cod. The air was still crisp with the dew of a cool, fall morning. Squinting in the glare of a glorious sunrise, I verified the number of the house and pulled into the driveway. The address on the paper matched the name taped onto the frosted mailbox. "Louis Cipher, Apartment #3." With just a car door and a couple of yards between us, I parked on the far side of the driveway and viewed the building that contained the aberrant parental mold from which my adolescence had been cast.

I could barely hear the gravel of the driveway crunching beneath my footsteps as I walked without reservation toward the door that insulated me from the assault of his stare. I had not permitted his icy, blue eyes to lay their demonic view upon me since I was 15 years old. My arm began to move in slow motion as I lifted my weighted hand and pressed my finger against the button of the doorbell. Seconds were protracted to hours as I waited in anticipation of his resuscitated hands to open the door. For a brief moment, I wondered how it was possible that I could have overcome the association, and fallen in love with the exquisite, blue pupils of Kurt's eyes.

"Yes?" a woman dressed in a white nurse's uniform answered from the inside of the screen door.

"Is Louis here?" I asked. Although the current of my blood was surging, I was immediately struck by how resolute I felt about my choice to meet with him.

"He's sleeping," she replied.

"Can you tell him that Terry is here?" I asked.

"Hold on," she said as she turned the corner into another room that was out of my view. Standing on the front porch outside of his door, squinting in the blinding morning sunlight, I reached down to pat the friendly greeting of his dog. For the very first time I could remember, the fear that preoccupied the hours of darkness throughout my life was notably absent.

I heard the soft, shuffle of footsteps and looked up to see a tall silhouette approaching through the screen. The door was opened by a skeletal version of the man that used to tower over me like Goliath.

"Well, look who's here," Louis said receptively, with a smile. His assumption that I was there for an affable reunion was obvious. He was clearly mistaken.

"Let's sit out on the porch and get some fresh air," he said.

"No, let's sit inside," I replied, surprised that I began our meeting with even the smallest act of defiance.

"O.K., come on in," Louis said as he led me into his living room. The door slammed shut behind me. I was on the inside. I felt the rush of adrenaline that burglars must feel once they penetrate the building they have staked out and planned to break into for years. Similarly, there was the respite after overcoming the first barrier, yet far from the relief of finishing the job.

I sat on the footstool of the chair and gazed upon the shell of a man sitting on the couch across from me. His dog licked my hand and affectionately curled up against my leg. As I reached down to scratch behind his ears, I felt it almost fitting, as I realized that Louis had been reduced to the company of an animal as his only remaining, single source of loving reverence.

"I heard you were having some health issues," I began as I recalled the e-mail I received the night before from my mother, informing me that she had heard his time had finally come.

"Yeah. I had a heart attack about five years ago and a quadruple bypass. They brought me back to life. Then I was diagnosed with stomach cancer a couple of years ago. The doctors tell me that I only have a week or two left to live. I hear you haven't had it so easy either." Louis said, attempting to commiserate with me as he alluded to whatever news he had heard about Kurt's demise.

"No, it wasn't easy," I replied. I refused to accept one moment of purported congeniality by spending any time discussing my woes about Kurt. "I got an e-mail from mom," I continued, immediately regretting the intimate reference of "mom" rather than the distant, more formalized title of "my mother" that would ordinarily be used with an outsider to family. Although I had thought about this moment for over 20 years, I hadn't scripted the dialogue. Continuing to rely on improvisation, I decided to keep going with instinct.

"I wanted to come here to tell you that I think you owe a lot of people an apology." It was evident that I was not there to offer him my condolences.

"The consequences of your behavior were far reaching. It wasn't just the people that you directly affected, like my mother or me. The people in our lives were impacted, too," I continued. Twenty-two years earlier and I would already be getting smashed up against the wall. Instead, age had destroyed the aggressor and stripped him of his power. If it weren't for the tone of his voice and the unforgettable, distinctive plague of his eyes, I wouldn't have believed whom I was gazing upon.

"Well, I've lived a lot more years than you, Terry. You can go through life holding onto things or you can move on," Louis replied.

"That's true. I agree. However, there are some things that happen in your life that stay with you forever, and it doesn't matter how much time passes. It could be 50 years later and it could still affect you like it just happened moments ago. It's like when your husband dies in your arms after four years of battling a horrible disease. The pain never really leaves you. Even though you manage not to dwell on it, and you go on with your life, you can call it up in a second. This is how I feel about you." Despite not having the slightest idea what response I would evoke from Louis, I daringly kept my tongue in motion. "For as long as I live, I will feel the agony of remembering the sounds of my mother whimpering and begging for you to stop beating her." Louis did not make a move.

"Those were bad times for all of us. I was taking drugs, your mother was taking drugs, and so were you," Louis said, surprisingly docile.

"I agree that they were bad times. But my mother was *not* taking drugs. I was there, Louis. She hates that stuff. She doesn't even drink," I defensively began, tempted to bury him with indisputable facts. But time was limited and I instead chose my battles more carefully. "I'm not going to make any excuses for myself. I will take full responsibility for my own decisions during my teens. Of course, the fact that you were the one giving me drugs didn't really help matters," I said, unable to resist firing in one last detail. The tension was palpable, but Louis didn't say a word. "But none of this has anything to do with why I came here," I resumed my focus. "You hurt a lot of people. You destroyed a family. It's not like an apology will take any of it away, but sometimes I've thought that it might be better to hear the words, rather than never hear them at all."

"Well, I, I, I do apologize," Louis stuttered.

Suddenly, I could feel myself losing my nerve. My heart relocated itself to my head, with each of my thoughts inhabited by their own pulse. The moment had come for me to choose whether I would turn around and leave, or brave going in for the kill. During my momentary debate, out of the corner of my eye, I caught a glimpse of a photo resting on top of a nearby shelf. There stood a framed, black and white photograph of Louis as a young, brawny man. He was standing shirtless in a pair of chinos with his arms draped around the shoulders of two women on either side of him. I recognized one of them to be his mother and the other his grandmother. Louis had played football as a kid. He towered over their small statures at about six feet tall and probably weighed in at a solid 220 pounds.

It was easy to be deceived by the decrepit and emaciated remains that sat on the couch before me. However, the eight-by-ten was just the sort of instant reminder I needed to remember that the body sitting before me still housed the demon in the photo. I unflinchingly turned the corner and went for it.

"So what about what you did to *me*?" I asked, staring directly into his eyes.

"What do you mean?" he asked almost inaudibly.

"What about what happened between you and me?" I repeated. Twenty-two years to consider it, and I still never dreamed I would ever have the courage or the opportunity to ask.

Louis hesitated for a few moments, clearly caught off guard. His body language spoke of his uneasiness, as he nervously moved his hands towards his face to scratch an itch that we both knew was not there.

"Well, I remember there was a lot of pampering," he quietly answered, as though wondering out loud.

"Pampering? *Pampering?*" Never raising my voice, I unhesitatingly emphasized my disbelief. "Do you call putting your hands down my pants almost every day for years *pampering*? Is that not *sexual* to you?" I squinted, tilting my head in astonishment.

"Me? What are you talking about? When?" Louis asked defiantly. I couldn't believe I actually had to answer the question, but I had come that far, and at that point, I was not going to let anything go.

"It was practically every day. Mostly when we were in the living room. You were in your easy chair in front of the television just before dinner, touching me under the pretense of giving me backrubs. You don't remember that?" I asked disbelievingly.

"No, I don't remember what you're talking about," Louis responded.

I had fantasized about a number of responses over the years. I always assumed he would shift the blame to me, but I had *never* predicted he would claim to forget. Grappling with an unforeseen reaction, I continued, led by nothing but pure emotion.

"For all these years you had me believing it was my fault. For *over 20 years*, I've asked myself why you did what you did. I've gone to professionals and asked them what you could've been thinking." I swallowed hard, and completely disregarded his attempted denial. "So, I'm asking you now. *What were you thinking?*"

"I don't remember any of that happening," Louis repeated, continuing to nervously fidget with his clothing.

"Do you know the effect that had on me? Do you know what it *still* does to me to this day?" I asked, dismissive of his response. Calm and monotone on the exterior, my insides were raging with the frustration that I would never get an answer to one of the most gnawing questions of my life. I was fully aware that no one would ever be able to proffer a rational explanation. But logic was no longer part of the equation. I had lived two decades with the desire to look him in the eyes and ask, as though for some reason, he might actually have had the ability to fulfill my need to know.

"Well, I apologize," Louis stammered, nervously raising his hand to his cheek once again. His anxious mannerisms alone were a partial victory.

"But your apology has hollow meaning if you don't even remember what you are apologizing for," I declared, once again, shocking myself with the ability to even speak to him in this manner without the fear of imminent harm. Age and poor health had finally declared open season.

"I don't know what happened to you when you were growing up, but obviously something terrible was going on in your house. I spent a lot of time with your mother when I was a kid, and she seemed nice enough. But something happened to make you do the things you did." Purely out of curiosity, I was tempted to provoke him into divulging some sort of childhood-abuse-excuse, but he wasn't even sharp enough to seize the opportunity, or try to exonerate himself.

"I've lived a lot of years, Terry. A lot more than you. Sometimes things happen between people and you keep it between you. But you chose to use how you felt about me, against me," Louis replied, insinuating he had somehow been unjustly persecuted by having his reputation slandered. Whatever the antithesis of guilt was began to occupy my entire body.

"Any lost relationships were decimated by *you*, Louis. *You* did that all on your own. And, anyone who cared about *me*, knowing what *you did* to me, would, of course, harbor those feelings as well," I began, gripped by a new tenacity. "But, myself aside, you inflicted enough harm on other people for their hatred to stand entirely on its own." It hadn't taken long for the flood of emotions to drown away my fear of braving my feelings. "If anything, I didn't say enough because I spent so many years of my life terrorized by the memories you left me with."

"Well, I hope you got whatever you needed by coming here." Louis spoke so uncharacteristically soft.

"I'm not sure, but I know that I needed to come here and see you once more, in order to tell you how I felt about what you did." The room fell silent. Suddenly, there was nothing more to say. Despite his deficient and unsatisfying responses, I realized that the true purpose of my visit had been accomplished. That is, to have *him* listen to *me* speak, not for me to listen to *him* speak. There were no answers worth hearing anymore.

"That's all I have to say to you," I announced, feeling another slight liberation from calling the last shot. "I'm going to leave now." I patted the welcoming dog on the head, stood up and walked back outside to a new day that at last, did not include a fear of Louis.

CHAPTER 30

The Final Lesson

October 2001

Sense memories come in all forms. Days before I was to step over the three-year threshold of Kurt's death, they were transported to me in the form of small, plastic bags of chocolates. Stop & Shop was not the venue where I had anticipated being broad-sided with his revival.

During the years following Kurt's funeral, I had bottled up selected feelings, and only occasionally took a sip from those memories. I would sometimes ease the passing aches of his absence by wearing his favorite t-shirt, or perhaps, biting into a slice of mango—a mainstay of his diet. Although it sometimes made me miss him even more, if the yearning became insufferable I would occasionally resort to the remedy of taking a sniff from the bottle of his favorite cologne.

Almost every year of my life, I enthusiastically waited for the earth to reorganize itself into the brilliant colors of a New England fall. Initially, the timing of Kurt's late September death had cushioned my grief. However, the crisp, sparkling air of my favorite season later became the conduit of hauntingly sorrowful memories.

Until the day I strolled down the supermarket's candy aisle, I had employed my standard strategy: Avoid the smells, sounds, and flavors of autumn's painful reminders. But this day was different. My new self-awareness conspired with the season and penetrated the fortitude of my senses. Shelves towered over me, crammed with seasonal, brown, orange, and yellow candy wrappers. The bones in my knuckles almost split through my skin as I gripped the handle of my shopping cart, and nearly dropped to my knees in the agony of my loss.

"So, it looks like the encore to seeking my pound of flesh from Louis is going to be the challenge of the fall," I began.

"What do you mean?" Cali asked.

"Well, I almost passed out from the pain of losing Kurt in the supermarket yesterday. I can't believe how the most innocuous things can trigger that much heartache. All I did was glance at the chocolates that are wrapped in fall colors, and bang, I felt like it was the day I walked out of Kurt's funeral. The fall may as well smell like his cologne at this point. I just wasn't prepared for it to become a painful reminder of him. Christ, Cali, it's been three years. Don't you think that's a bizarre reaction?"

"Not at all. It's called grieving, Terry. Again, all the feelings you avoided were merely postponed, not eliminated. Of course the fall is going to remind you of how you felt when Kurt died. More than likely, you will experience a lot of conflicting emotions because you are so much more awake now."

"*That* is *not* very good news," I replied.

"I know, Terry," Cali sympathetically agreed. "But, as we've discussed over and over again, you *cannot* make your feelings go away. I once heard something really insightful about loss that I've never forgotten: Often the pain doesn't become less intense, but it *does* become less frequent. And, Terry, when it arrives you will now have the tools to deal with it. You never have to be alone with how you're feeling again. Can you see this?"

"Yeah, I understand, and I hope you're right. But I still don't get how I can feel such pain during some periods of time, and then such anger during others. I know it wasn't his choice, but that doesn't stop me from being mad at Kurt for leaving me, or mad that I'm alone and having to start my life all over again."

"It's not unusual for people who have experienced loss to feel both emotions at the same time. Anger and pain can co-exist. Much like the other conflicting emotions we've discussed, missing Kurt and being angry because he left you are not mutually exclusive," Cali explained. "But the positive feelings *will* become more prevalent over time, and someday, you may even love the fall again."

"But, if I continue to feel this way, how will I know when my grieving turns into dwelling?"

"Don't worry, Terry, I'll let you know if you start dwelling on anything," Cali laughed. "I don't think you run the risk of overplaying things. In fact, you're on the other end of the extreme. How many times have you protested something about your childhood because you didn't '*specifically*' remember it?" she teased. "You haven't even allowed yourself to *start* thinking about things, never mind think about them too much. There is a balance between facing things and dwelling on them. Let's just try to get you to feel first. Okay?"

"Well, that's just great. Now that I'm awake, I get to *inhale* Kurt's fall cologne every time I step outside," I sarcastically responded. "Yeah, okay, okay, I see your point," I conceded. "But, do you want to know what all of this *really* feels like?"

"Yes," Cali replied.

"It feels like losing Kurt was an *emotional amputation*, and sometimes, I don't know if I'll ever be able to adapt to it."

"But many people who become amputees learn to overcome their losses, and find ways to replace what they originally had. It's never *exactly* the same, but that doesn't mean there isn't another way that can't work just as well."

"You mean that I should find an emotional prosthetic?" I joked.

"Yes," Cali beamed. "You *will* meet someone again, Terry," she reassured me.

"But, *you don't know* that. There is *no way* you can know that for sure," I wistfully replied. "In my heart of hearts, I truly believe that I will never be able to fall in love again."

"You are right, *neither* one of us really knows for certain. But, as much as you *don't* believe it, I *do* believe it, and therefore, I have just as much chance as you of being right," Cali persuasively explained.

"I admit that you have a point. But I find it hard to believe I will ever find anyone I love as much as Kurt."

"The man you meet definitely won't be Kurt. He will be different, but that doesn't mean your relationship can't be just as good. Despite your convictions that you won't feel that way again, someday you will see that you absolutely will. And, when you choose, you'll bring your gifts to another person who can love and care for you. You are just waking up to the world, Terry. Give yourself some time. You have so much life ahead of you to look forward to."

"I'm working on having more faith, Cali. I really don't want to be alone forever," I said. "I'm trying to focus on the times that I've begun to feel better lately. Even though what happened yesterday in the supermarket was painful, I weathered it much better than I ever would have before."

"What did you do to get through it?"

"Well, first I sat in my car, in the supermarket's parking lot, and sobbed my eyes out. But when I started to settle down a little bit, I called a friend and treated myself to a dinner out. The pain didn't go away, but it definitely didn't paralyze me like it used to either."

"That's *incredible*, Terry. You are learning how to reach out, and take care of yourself. Do you see how far you've come since Christmas?"

"Yeah. Maybe in the future, I won't wait until I have a flesh wound before taking my head off the chopping block," I smiled. "I don't know what I would have done without you, Cali. You've done so much for me. In fact, now that I think about it, you probably undercharged me."

"Oh Terry, I couldn't have gotten anywhere without your commitment to honesty, and your willingness to listen, and consider other perspectives. You came in here, and *you* did the work. In fact, now that *I* think about it, I was probably overpaid."

Warmed by the notion, I responded with a gleaming smile.

"Well, whether or not you want to take any of the credit, you jumped inside of me and burrowed yourself so deep that many of the monsters had to move aside. There aren't many people who would have done that."

"I am not the exception, Terry. I'm just a person you allowed into your life, and there are others just like me, waiting for you to love and trust them. Don't you get that, yet?"

"It's still hard for me, but I am *really* working on it," I said. "You once told me that even if I didn't have hope for the future, you would hope for both of us until I could," I continued. "That really helped to carry me during those times. I've learned a lot from you and this process, including having the faith that things could change."

"What has changed for you?" Cali asked.

"I learned *not* to walk away, and how staying could actually be worth it. I'm glad I couldn't make you *not* matter. I also learned a lot about honesty, loyalty and compromise."

"What else have you learned?" she continued.

"You once asked me to define what therapy was, and I said that it was so many things that it defied explanation. But, I think I've finally learned how to describe it."

"Really?" Cali responded with pleasure. "How would you describe it?"

"It's a *process*. It's not a succession of isolated appointments. It's like every session becomes part of a stream of infinite sequels to the last."

"Geez, that's a great way of describing it. Anything else?"

"Well, it was important for me to make a firm commitment to the process—even if it required enduring periods when I was skeptical, and had to rely on a blind, trusting faith that there would be benefits down the road. Then again, benefiting from the process was not entirely dependent upon an all-or-nothing commitment, or talking about the past. I still learned a lot, even when I had one foot out the door. Like when Kurt was alive and I refused to talk about the past, and never knew if I was going to continue coming in or not. It was still useful to work on the present, and it's what helped me make some changes, including getting some help with his care before I dropped dead of exhaustion."

"Yes. That was a difficult time. I understood the position you were in, but I was frustrated I couldn't do more to help you. I'm so glad you got some help at home."

"Yeah, me too," I agreed. "Probably, the most important thing about the process has been learning to believe in change. It took me a while to have any faith in the transposition of thoughts. Even when I didn't believe change was possible, I had to learn how to trust you to guide me, and believe that whenever there seem to be no answers, there are always possibilities as long as we keep talking."

"Oh Terry. Look how far you've come. Do you see it? Do you *really* see it?"

"Yeah, I do. Sometimes, I don't feel like I'm really out of the woods, but I guess I have to accept that life will never be a utopia, and that *I* will always be a work in progress."

"Well, there's still a very important lesson for you to learn. And, once you understand it, you will *never* lose it. Do you know what that is?" Cali asked.

"No, I have no idea," I replied.

"I want you to think about it. It's something *no one* will ever be able to take away from you."

"Come on, Cali," I whined. "Can't you, *just once*, tell me something without the torture of making me answer first?"

"No," Cali quipped, with a big smile across her face.

"Why am I not surprised?" I joked. "I really don't know, Cali. Really."

"It has to do with how you feel about yourself," she generously hinted.

I was too intrigued to fight her any further. My mind ran through a list of possibilities like a ticker tape. "You mean accepting that I'm a loser?" I smirked.

"Very funny, Terry. *You know* what the lesson is," Cali pushed me to say the words.

"Okay, okay," I stalled. "It's about liking myself."

"Yes. If you learn to like yourself, whatever people say or do might influence you, but they will never be able to take that away."

"What do you mean?" I asked.

"Well, for example, if you were very tall, but someone called you short, or vice versa, you would laugh, and shrug them off, because *you* would know they were wrong. It's the same thing with liking yourself. If you believe in yourself, it won't matter if others think differently about you. And, it will help sustain you during the times that life deals you difficulties. You *will* find the comfort that you've been seeking."

"I *am* feeling more comfortable with myself," I replied. "Except when I'm at work."

"I agree. You started off so happy working there, but you haven't seemed that way for a while. I've never believed there is only *one* job for a person. You need to like what you do, and yes, Terry, it *is* possible despite what you're thinking."

"But nothing I've ever done has held my interest. It seems rather spoiled for me to expect that I could actually enjoy my job."

"So, in other words, if you really enjoy your work, you are lazy, or taking the easy way out? You know, Terry, it's not like you are *cheating* if you find something that you love to do."

"Wow. You're right. It does feel like I'm cheating if I'm too happy with work. It's like my job has to feel like *work* in order for it to be okay," I agreed, feeling a monumental twist in my perspective.

"The only time I've seen your eyes really light up has been when you've talked to me about how much you love to write. Why don't you try doing something with that?" Cali suggested.

"But writing has only been a hobby and that's much different than writing for work. I don't think I can do it, Cali," I hesitantly replied. The idea began to flicker.

"You won't know what you're capable of until you give it a try. *Your* way ensures that you will *never* become a writer. At some point, you have to believe in yourself enough to take risks."

"Well, I'd *really* love it if I could do something like that." Despite my initial reservation, her suggestion would ultimately become the round peg that would fit the hole in my lifelong search for personal comfort and a passion for my work. I could already feel a surge of irrepressible excitement igniting inside of me.

I turned to Cali with a smile. "So, what do you think I should write about?"

Epilogue

Ten Years Later

July 2010

Dear Reader,

Ten years ago, I couldn't imagine why anyone would want to live, and I was surrounded by people who couldn't imagine why anyone would want to die. In the years that have passed since *Waking Up* was first published, my life has transformed. I no longer have to strain my imagination to feel joy or happiness. I can't say I found the panacea to counter all of life's challenges. Instead, I learned that being emotionally healthy means feeling everything fully and possessing the coping skills to manage life's downturns. But first let me focus on the upturns, many of which I never anticipated would result from writing *Waking Up*.

Shortly after the release of *Waking Up* in 2004, I embarked on what I refer to as my "accidental public speaking career." I did not realize that the book would have such a widespread impact, but soon found myself standing before a diversity of audiences who were hungry to find a way out of their darkness. I have since delivered hundreds of speeches nationwide to provide inspiration to those in need and tools to those who help them. It is hard for me to grasp that the depressed and introverted 10-year-old little girl I once was now stands before hundreds of people doing an emotional striptease. But here I am, clothed in the fulfillment I get every time I learn that something I said or wrote helped someone.

There is a wall in my office at home papered with letters, each of which provides me with another dose of inspiration to continue my efforts. It took a long time to figure out why so many people thanked me. Countless letters and e-mails later, I began to understand. People were looking for something that I had also been searching for and was fortunate enough to find: Hope and the ability to cope. Yet I don't think my audiences are aware of how much they've given to me.

Recently, I was delivering a keynote speech and I spontaneously decided to say something that I have never said to any other audience. As I talked about the many things that helped me recover and regain hope, I revealed that one of them was that I had found love again. I was stunned by the loud applause that broke out across the entire auditorium. Until then, I hadn't fully appreciated how important it was for people to see that despite the most ill-fated past, life can go on and joy can return. It was as if my falling in love again was a shared victory. It is one that I will continue to celebrate.

Sometimes I wonder if people think that just because I wrote *Waking Up*, and because I am so actively involved in advocating for mental health, that I never face downturns. However, there are times when loneliness still creeps up on me, a lack of self-esteem still challenges me, and grief periodically haunts me. I recognize that I am at increased risk for recurrent depression. But there is a big difference between 10 years ago and now. I now understand that those feelings won't last forever (which is critical to avoid feeling hopeless) and I know that I must reach out for help. Admittedly, I still have a tendency to retreat, but I remind myself of the importance of talking about how I am feeling.

One of the most critical lessons I learned is that emotional health does not mean being happy all the time. It means possessing the coping skills to manage a wide range of emotions. Life no longer feels like an endurance test and I live each day like it's my first, not my last. I work hard to keep a balance in my life. I enjoy kayaking, hiking, pressing one for more options, watching sports, and observing the on-going battle between the left and right sides of my brain. I still have a few lofty goals: Getting Oprah Winfrey to add *Waking Up* to her top ten favorite books, banning phone menu systems, figuring out why phonetic is not spelled with an "f," and dispelling the myth that you can't have your cake and eat it, too.

One last update: Dr. Cali Joseph (a.k.a. Dr. Betsy Glaser) and I finished treatment in 2001. We have since co-presented at various conferences, as well as at clinical psychology programs where *Waking Up* is required reading. It is a rare opportunity for audiences to hear from both sides of the couch. Dr. Joseph does live on in another capacity. She is a central character in my first novel, which I recently completed. Even in the world of fiction, she is brilliant.

The week before *Waking Up* was first published, my best friend said something that spun me on my heels. She said to me, "If you help one person with this book, it was worth it—even if that person is you." Truer words were never spoken.

Best Regards,

Terry

Resources

Terry L. Wise, J.D., Author & Public Speaker,
www.TerryWise.com

SUICIDE PREVENTION HOTLINES

National Suicide Prevention Lifeline, 800-273-TALK (8255),
www.suicidepreventionlifeline.org

The Samaritans, 877-870-HOPE (4673),
www.samaritanshope.org

Samariteens - Teen Helpline, 800-252-TEEN (8336),
www.samaritanshope.org/samariteens.html

**Veterans: National Suicide Prevention Lifeline,
800-273-TALK (8255),** Press 1,
www.suicidepreventionlifeline.org

SUICIDE PREVENTION RESOURCES

Active Minds on Campus, www.ActiveMinds.org

American Association of Suicidology, www.suicidology.org

American Foundation for Suicide Prevention, www.afsp.org

Befrienders Worldwide, www.befrienders.org

The Jed Foundation, www.JedFoundation.org

The National Council for Suicide Prevention, www.ncsp.org

**National Empowerment Center, Inc., Directory of
Consumer-Run State-Wide Organizations,**
www.power2u.org/consumerrun-statewide.html

National Organization for People of Color Against Suicide,
www.nopcas.com

**Substance Abuse & Mental Health Services Administration
(SAMHSA), National Mental Health Information
Center,** http://mentalhealth.samhsa.gov

Suicide Awareness Voices of Education (SAVE),
www.save.org

Suicide Prevention Action Network USA (SPAN),
www.spanusa.org

Suicide Prevention Resource Center, www.sprc.org

**Suicide Prevention Resource Center:
Safe & Effective Messaging for Suicide Prevention,**
www.sprc.org/library/SafeMessagingfinal.pdf

Trevor Project, 866-4-U-TREVOR (88-7386),
www.TheTrevorProject.org

**U.S. Department of Veterans Affairs (*Mental Health and
Suicide Prevention),** www.MentalHealth.va.gov/
suicide_prevention/index.asp

Wounded Warrior Project,
www.WoundedWarriorProject.com